EXPLORE OSCAR® SEASON -

CHART A PATH TO THE ACADEMY AWARDS®

DISCOVER HOW MOVIES VIE FOR AN OSCAR®

The Only Oscar® Season Guide for Academy Award® Fans

BY CATHERINE R. LESTER

Explore Oscar® Season: Chart a Path to the Academy Awards®

Written by Catherine R. Lester

ISBN: 978-0-578-62452-5 paperback

Library of Congress Control Number 2019920577

Cover Design by rebecacovers

Edited by Lydia K. Ingram

Author portrait by Tammy Lechner

Revised Edition - 2023

Publisher: Company Voice Box LLC.

TABLE OF CONTENTS

DEDICATION v
INTRODUCTION vii

OSCAR SEASON – PHASE I
MOVIE PREMIERES AT FILM FESTIVALS

CHAPTER 1 – OSCAR SEASON 1
FILM FESTIVALS 2
CASE IN POINT 6
EARLY CAMPAIGNING 6

OSCAR SEASON – PHASE II
FILMS' PRECEDING AWARDS
IMPLY OSCAR WORTHINESS

CHAPTER 2 – ELIGIBILITY 13
ACADEMY AWARD RULES 14
PRECEDING FILM AWARDS 26

OSCAR SEASON – PHASE III
ACADEMY AWARD NOMINEES SELECTED

CHAPTER 3 – GETTING NOMINATED 35
PRELIMINARY VOTING 35
DETERMINING NOMINEES 41
CHAPTER 4 – NOMINEES REVEALED 43
NOMINATIONS ANNOUNCED 43
SNUBS AND FLUBS 44
CAMPAIGNING 50
CHAPTER 5 – SELECTING OSCAR WINNERS 53
AMPAS'S VIEWING PREFERENCE 53
PREFERENTIAL VOTING 55
VOTER BIAS AND VOTING BODY 58
CHAPTER 6 – EXCITEMENT BUILDS 63

OTHER AMPAS AWARDS....63
OSCAR NOMINEE LUNCHEON....66
OSCAR WEEK....66
STARS ANNOUNCED....67

OSCAR SEASON – THE BIG REVEAL ACADEMY AWARDS ACTIVITIES

CHAPTER 7 – OSCAR NIGHT....71
THE HOST....71
THE RED CARPET....75
BEHIND THE SCENES....78
AWARD RECIPIENTS....80
VIEWERSHIP....84
GOVERNORS BALL....85
OSCAR PARTIES....87
CHAPTER 8 – DO OSCAR NIGHT RIGHT....89
THREE-STEP PREP....90
SWAG....96
PLAN FOR NEXT YEAR....97
ABOUT THE AUTHOR....99
RESOURCES....101

DEDICATION

To Cray Daniel and Mayle –
Great things happen when you do things you love.

HONORING

David Rubin –
I have you to thank for my Oscar obsession, which began with Ralph Fiennes in The English Patient.

INTRODUCTION

My fascination with the Academy Awards stems from watching movies that have been nominated for a best picture Academy Award. As an Oscar fan, I have fun seeing the nominees in this category, and deciding for myself which should win an Academy Award. Every year, I get more and more into it, curious to know details about how it all happens and how I can be a part of the action. Over the years, I have found a wealth of information regarding the nomination and voting process, and Academy Award events that are open to the public.

My immense interest, which has spanned more than two decades, has yielded golden opportunities that most Academy Award fans don't know exist. I've participated in numerous official Oscar events without clout or special credentials. My fan experience includes Oscars Red Carpet Fan Experience, Oscar Week, Oscar Concert, and attending the grand opening of the Academy Museum of Motion Pictures in Los Angeles; and Oscar Roadtrip and Oscar Fan Experience in Texas. I'm also a founding donor of the Academy Museum of Motion Pictures.

A few years ago, it occurred to me: what good are these experiences if I keep them to myself? Having researched, studied, and validated resources, I know what's available for Academy Award fans. For me, the Oscars are more exciting than Christmas, and believing that the millions of Academy Award viewers feel the same way compels me to share knowledge to heighten their experience. This book introduces you to Oscar Season, which starts months before the Academy Awards ceremony.

Oscar Season is a phenomenon that professionals in the movie industry know about and talk about, but it was not formally recognized by the Academy of Motion Picture Arts and Sciences (AMPAS) until recently. Oscar Season has existed for decades, however AMPAS claimed it in 2021 when promoting Global Film Day on February 13, 2021. If you were to go to the Academy's library and ask for rules or guidelines about Oscar Season, you would find only one press release for a 2021 social media kit that mentions the launch of the 93rd Oscar Season prompted by Global Movie Day; yet it clearly exists. Film studios, movie critics, and film awards analysts believe Oscar Season starts in the late summer when movies premiere at prominent film festivals. There is also an understanding among these industry professionals that Oscar Season happens in two phases: before Academy Award nominations and after nominations. My findings indicate there are three phases: (1) in the summer when major film festivals begin, (2) in the fall when other award ceremonies honor films released that year, and (3) in the winter when the Oscar nominations are announced.

My goal for writing this book is to engage you in the process and inspire you to move forward with your Academy Awards journey, whether that is attending a film festival, watching other award ceremonies, or seeing nominated films in a particular category. As of this publication date, no other published fan guide about Oscar Season exists. Now, with this book in hand, you now have the intel to make this the best Oscar Season ever.

OSCAR SEASON – PHASE I

MOVIE PREMIERES AT FILM FESTIVALS

CHAPTER 1 – OSCAR SEASON

Most people think Academy Award season begins when the Oscar nominations are announced—typically in January. However, the buzz about Oscar-worthy films begins several months before. Although the Academy of Motion Picture Arts and Sciences (AMPAS) declare the launch of Oscar Season on Global Movie Day, industry professionals consider Labor Day weekend as the start.

At the beginning of Oscar Season, most of the activity happens at film festivals where film studios are launching movie premieres. Studios prefer to release their Oscar-worthy films in the third or fourth quarter of the year—as close as possible to Academy Award nominations consideration. Studios want their movies to be fresh in the minds of AMPAS members who vote for films to be on the ballot. Chapter 3 has details about the nomination process.

Some filmmakers use the festival circuit for publicity purposes, though others are out to win festival prizes. AMPAS is a sponsor for many well-known film festivals, and the organization has sanctioned numerous film festivals that serve as qualifying events for Academy Award consideration in the documentary and short film categories. The major film festivals that occur in the late summer and fall each year, listed below, are considered showcase venues for mainstream Oscar categories. So when you see news about well-received movies that launched at any of these festivals, pay attention because the Oscar buzz is starting.

FILM FESTIVALS

Telluride Film Festival

For more than four decades, the Telluride Film Festival, presented by the National Film Preserve, has been happening over Labor Day weekend in Telluride, Colorado. Known as a low-key festival patronized by high-profile talent, the Telluride Film Festival is unique because there are no red carpets, juries, or prizes, and the program lineup is kept under wraps until a day or so before the festival begins. Big budget films and independent movies, such as *Darkest Hour* (1997) and *Nomadland* (2020) have debuted there and have gone on to earn Oscar nominations for best picture and other categories.

Venice Film Festival

The Venice Film Festival in Italy also takes place each year at the beginning of September. This festival, which began in 1932, certainly has all the glitz and glamour expected from a truly international affair. Some American production companies use this platform to premiere their films to the world. Red carpet events and press conferences occur daily. A golden lion statuette is awarded to winners of the film competition. *The Shape of Water*, directed by Guillermo Del Toro, won the Golden Lion award in 2017, then went onto earn 13 Oscar nominations, winning four Academy Awards, including best picture. Movies like *Gravity* (2013),*Birdman* (2015) made their world premiere at the Venice Film Festival, eventually making a mark in Academy Awards history. *Gravity* won 8 out of 10 Oscar nominations, including best director. *Birdman* won four out of nine Oscar nominations, including best picture.

Toronto International Film Festival

The Toronto International Film Festival in Ontario, Canada, has been running since 1976 and is the ideal venue for filmmakers to premiere their movies in North America. It presents jury awards in several categories, with the Grolsch People's Choice Award being the most coveted. In 2021, *Belfast* made its North American screening in Toronto before going on to earn six Oscar nominations, winning an Academy Award for original screenplay by Kenneth Branagh, writer, and director.

New York Film Festival

The New York Film Festival, which typically spans two weeks, is a platform for films, mainly international, to make their U.S. premiere. Founded in 1963 by Film at Lincoln Center, a branch of the world-renowned Lincoln Center, this festival showcases feature films, documentaries, and short films, and hosts panel discussions and film revivals. In 2021, *Drive My Car,* was screened at this event before earning four Oscar nominations, including best picture and winning one Academy Award for best international feature film.

AFI Fest

The American Film Institute (AFI), based out of Los Angeles, hosts its festival in early fall and is a platform for movie premieres, as well as screenings of international, short, classic and first-time director films. Founded in 1967, AFI festival includes galas, an educational summit and it awards prizes to 10 films, 10 television programs, and a special Life Achievement Award to an industry professional. In 2019, *Joker* was screened at this event before earning eleven Oscar nominations and winning two Academy Awards.

Other Film Festivals

Festivals that occur in the first quarter of the year appear to be vibrant marketplaces for studios to purchase films rather than promote them. For example, in 2019, Warner Bros./New Line purchased *Blinded by the Light* for $15 million at the Sundance Film Festival. At the same event, Netflix spent $33 million on three movies, and Amazon purchased five films for $47 million. The implication is that expensive movie buys are the mark of exceptional films, so consider that to be a prelude to the nomination buzz those movies may garner later.

Movies that premiere at film festivals in the winter, spring, or summer still have a shot at being recognized as Oscar-worthy; however, studios must coordinate promotional efforts at the right times to bring attention back to their films months after their initial release. Prominent film festivals to keep your eye on include:

Sundance Film Festival

The Sundance Film Festival takes place primarily in Park City, Utah, in late January, only a couple of weeks before Oscar nominations are announced. This festival gives jury prizes in numerous film categories, and it has panel discussions and a variety of film-related activities. The Sundance Institute has hosted this festival since 1985, and most film fans recognize it as Robert Redford's film fest. It's seldom that films that premiere here go onto be Oscar nominated but *CODA* (2021) made its debut here and won Best Picture.

Berlin International Film Festival

The Berlin International Film Festival was launched early in the Cold War to showcase the free world to the Berlin community through film. Since its inception in 1951, the festival has evolved into a major event. Spanning approximately 11 days in February, this festival hosts premieres and competitions, and it has events for directors making their debut.

SXSW

Since 1987, Austin, Texas, is where many filmmakers have spent their spring break. What makes South by Southwest (SXSW) special is that the film festival occurs adjacent to tech, music, and comedy festivals. Thus, movie makers are surrounded by an even broader creative bunch. SXSW's film festival takes place in March, typically over eight days, and it's a qualifying event for the Academy Awards short film category. *Everything Everywhere All at Once* (2022) is the only film that has premiered at SXSW and went onto earn an Academy Award Best Picture honor.

Tribeca Film Festival

Occurring in April in New York City, the Tribeca Film Festival was established in 2001 as a venue for dynamic independent films to expand viewership. Hosted by Tribeca Enterprises, and founded by Robert De Niro, Jane Rosenthal, and Craig Hatkoff, this festival takes place over a 12-day period after the Oscars have concluded.

Cannes Film Festival

The regal city of Cannes, France, has hosted the Cannes Film Festival for over 70 years. Known internationally, this 12-day festival occurs in May and has made its mark as a prestigious, glamourous, and star-studded event. *Parasite* (2019) made its premiere here and later earned the Best Picture Oscar in 2020.

Qualifying Festivals

In addition to helping a film garner attention, festivals can also help certain types of films become eligible for an Oscar nomination. Each of the 23 Academy Award categories has eligibility requirements, and those requirements differ by category. For example, the requirements for directing will be different than sound editing. There is a unique provision for films in the categories of documentary feature, documentary short subject, short film live action, and animated short film. AMPAS allows those films to achieve eligibility in three different ways, one being to win a qualifying award at a competitive film festival. A current list of qualifying festivals is available at www.oscars.org on the Awards webpage, in the Rules & Eligibility section.

CASE IN POINT

Why are film festivals such a big deal? They're a way for studios to introduce their movies to the world and get industry professionals talking about them. They want word of their films to spread among the film community and reach voting members of the Academy and other prominent award programs, such as the Golden Globes and the British Academy of Film and Television Arts (BAFTA). In short, Academy members are scanning film festival news about well-received films, which helps them determine which movies are worthy of their time, attention, and nomination consideration.

According to www.screendaily.com, of the 106 Oscar nominations across all feature film categories in 2019, 39 nominated films (36.8 percent) had been screened at the 2018 Venice Film Festival, and 13 films (12 percent) had been screened at the 2018 Cannes Film Festival.

Fewer of the 2019 Oscar-nominated films premiered at film festivals in North America in 2018. A total of 21 nominated films were screened at U.S. and Canadian festivals: 9 stemming at the Toronto Film Festival, 4 in Telluride, 4 at the Sundance Film Festival, 2 at SXSW, and 2 at the AFI Festival.

EARLY CAMPAIGNING

Campaigning and Oscar Season go together. Not only do studios make plans to market their Oscar-worthy films to movie-goers, but they also have a master plan to get their films nominated for Academy Awards. When it comes to campaigning an Oscar hopeful, film studios, distributors, and marketing companies must all follow the same set of campaign rules governed by AMPAS. To level the playing field, AMPAS campaign regulations relay descriptions of activities that are and are not permissible.

Although members of the Academy of Motion Picture Arts and Sciences are supposed to evaluate a movie based solely on its artistic and technical merits, it is possible for them to be swayed. AMPAS regulations have evolved over time, but there was a time when members were given tokens of appreciation and invited by A-list celebrities to attend elaborate parties. Interestingly, studios had access to Academy members' home addresses and would mail screeners and promotional materials directly to them. There was a long period of time when film companies had a robust contact list of Academy members to solicit during Oscar Season. Awards consultants benefitted the most from those lists because they would sell them to studios that had a potential nominee. However, in 2018, AMPAS adopted a new process whereby a mailing house would receive materials and then distribute those materials to AMPAS members who opted in. In 2020, AMPAS changed its screener policy to discontinue the distribution of DVD screeners beginning with the 94th Academy Awards, for films released in 2021. AMPAS has a private online platform to store eligible films for members to consider for nomination, therefore this new policy supports their sustainability efforts.

AMPAS is very protective of its members, and it restricts how studios can engage voters in their campaigns. For example, Academy members may attend official screening events and private film events but there is to be no outward demonstration of their support or endorsement for that movie if they are not directly associated with it. No promotional materials or anything of value may be given to members at screenings or elsewhere. Academy members not directly associated with the film in any form of advertising are allowed to be quoted or make comments, a reversal ruling made in 2020.Governors or committee members are prohibited from commenting on films.

AMPAS publishes its awards campaign promotional regulations every summer, that are applicable to that year's film releases and it publishes its complete rules, and key dates for the next Academy Awards simultaneously. The campaign promotional regulations gives details of activities that are and are not permissible. Campaigning movies during Oscar Season is a hot topic because studios find ways to work around the regulations. The complete rules, a different document, is a comprehensive guideline per branch (acting, cinematography, etc.) on the requirements films need to be eligible for Oscars consideration. Chapter 2 covers this in detail. The key dates, a different document, give advance notice of nomination and voting deadlines for members, shortlist announcement date, and the dates for the Governors Awards, nominee luncheon, and of course, the Academy Awards ceremony. These documents can be found on AMPAS's website, in the News section.

The most well-known Oscar campaign stunt known among movie professionals is when Harvey Weinstein pitched *Shakespeare in Love* (1998) to Academy Award voters by telephone. In 1999, when Harvey Weinstein was Miramax co-chief, he was competing in the best picture race against DreamWorks's Steven Spielberg. Although there were other films nominated in this category, *Shakespeare in Love* (1998) and *Saving Private Ryan* (1998) were the frontrunners. To push *Shakespeare in Love* across the finish line, Weinstein called Academy members to confirm receipt of the screener and engaged in conversation about his film while simultaneously disparaging *Saving Private Ryan*. His tactics seemingly paid off, as *Shakespeare in Love* won best picture; however, the resulting controversy tainted the win. Thereafter, AMPAS updated their campaign rules to specifically prohibited telephone lobbying.

This ruling played out in 2014, when composer Bruce Brougton's song "Alone Yet Not Alone" was nominated for an Academy Award in the best song category. Broughton, himself an Academy member, excitedly emailed members of the AMPAS Music Branch asking for their consideration. Broughton's actions compelled AMPAS to disqualify the song and replace it with another nominee.

AMPAS campaign regulations draw a clear distinction between campaigning prior to the announcement of nominations and campaigning after nominees have been revealed. Before the nomination process begins, AMPAS is a bit more lenient about campaigning, allowing studios to engage in certain activities with its members. For example, before nominees are determined, AMPAS members may be invited to screenings that serve reasonable food and beverage. After nominations are announced, however, screenings can't include food, beverage, entertainment, or other forms of hospitality. The term "reasonable" is open to interpretation. If film companies break the rules, their films may get disqualified.

Prior to 2023, this rule did not prevent AMPAS members from hosting parties for their nominated friends nor does it prohibit them from posting shout outs on social media. These tactics were clearly visible during the 2022-2023 Oscar Season when famous people did just that. AMPAS members, Jodie Foster, Jake Gyllenhaal and Melanie Griffith threw a party for best supporting actress nominee, Jamie Lee Curtis. A different party was hosted for Michelle Yeoh best actress nominee, and was attended by AMPAS members. Both actresses were awarded an Oscar for the same film. The most talked about social media campaign that year was the promotion of Andrea Riseborough as a best actress nominee. A-list talent, Reese Witherspoon, Kate Winslet, and Charlize Theron praised Riseborough for her acting in *To Leslie* (2022) on social media prior to the Academy Award nominations. Riseborough was not well-known at the time, and it was a shock when she was announced as a nominee. Some believed her campaign, orchestrated by the film director's wife, Mary McCormack, crossed the line, and in spite of complaints to AMPAS, no corrective action was taken that campaign season. Their rules changed in May 2023, when campaign regulations included guidelines for social media posts. Academy members are prohibited from posting encouraging or discouraging messages about eligible films and potential nominees, an implied corrective action from the Riseborough incident. AMPAS reviews the campaign regulations and complete rules annually and updates them as needed.

OSCAR SEASON – PHASE II

FILMS' PRECEDING AWARDS IMPLY OSCAR WORTHINESS

CHAPTER 2 – ELIGIBILITY

For movies to be considered for an Academy Award, they must meet criteria established by AMPAS. The requirements for each Oscar category are different. Technically, there are 24 Academy Award categories; however, nominees are typically determined for 23 categories because the 24th category—original musical—rarely has films to consider. Best original musical was established in 2000, but as of this publication date, no nominations have been made and no award has been given for this category although there have been musicals released since then.

AMPAS has a rule book for every Academy Awards year. Typically, AMPAS's Board of Governors meets in the spring, after the Oscars have concluded, to review the existing rules and to determine if changes are needed. For example, in 2019, the number of nominees in the Makeup and Hairstyling category was increased from three to five, and the foreign language film category name was changed to international feature film. In 2020, a rule for best picture changed to nominating a set of ten films versus a fluctuating number of at least five with a maximum of ten. Once changes are approved, AMPAS publishes the official Oscar rules for the next awards program. In 2023, the rules for best picture included AMPAS's Representation and inclusion (RAISE) requirements. The rules are available to the public and are posted on www.oscars.org, in the Awards webpage, under "Oscars." A summary of changes is included in a press release, when the new rules are posted, that is also located on AMPAS's website.

Of the existing 27 rules, rules 1 through 5 apply to all filmmakers submitting their work for consideration. Rules 6 through 27 are specific to individual categories and to the Governors Awards, Special Achievement Awards, and the Scientific and Technical Special Awards. For filmmakers who dream of producing an Oscar-worthy movie, these rules are an excellent guide for knowing what's expected. Here is an overview of some of the major rules for the 96th Academy Awards (May 1, 2023).

ACADEMY AWARD RULES

Rule 1: Awards Definitions

This rule specifies that the Academy Awards ceremony occurs annually, and the 24 award categories are listed for each branch. Some awards for specific categories may not be given every year. This rule also states individual awards within the Governors Awards program and the Special Awards program may not be given each year, even though those awards programs occur annually.

Rule 2: Eligibility

This rule covers the technical requirements for films and screening criteria. A movie is considered to be a feature film if it is 40 minutes in length or longer, and if the moving image (film or digital) meets specific resolution criteria for picture and sound quality. Screening requirements can change, as we experienced during the COVID-19 pandemic. Typically, films are screened in a commercial cinema in cities within Los Angeles County and other select cities nationwide for a minimum of seven consecutive days, with at least three showings per day for paid admission. This rule also states screenings are to be documented and submitted with a list of the film's credits. During the COVID-19 pandemic in 2022-2021, AMPAS amended this rule, but has returned to its standard operating procedures.

There are different eligibility requirements for animated feature films, documentaries, international feature films, music awards, and short films. Those requirements are stated in the rules for those specific categories.

The rule regarding eligibility came to the forefront of entertainment news in 2019 when Netflix's *Roma* (2018) earned 10 Oscar nominations, include best picture. This recognition for a streaming film angered industry professionals because die-hard cinema filmmakers believed *Roma* was created for a streaming platform and not for a theatrical platform. Steven Spielberg came forward after the Academy Awards in 2019, in the name of cinematic art and science to declare that *Roma* was made for mobile devices, not cinema and should, therefore, not qualify as a motion picture. Spielberg suggested rule 2's theatrical screening in LA County requirement be increased, suggesting a four-week period. AMPAS's Board of Governors had a special session to discuss the issue and invited cinema leaders and industry professionals to weigh in on the future of cinema. The discussion resulted in no change to rule 2; the one-week requirement remained.

AMPAS doesn't ignore streaming as a vital channel; rule 2 allows filmmakers to distribute a film on nontheatrical media on or after the film's first day in a Los Angeles County theater. However, rule 2 clearly states that if the film is exhibited on nontheatrical media before the movie is shown in a theater, then it doesn't qualify. This rule applies to feature films; but the other genres, like shorts and international features, have different guidelines. "Nontheatrical" is defined as internet transmission, pay-per-view, video-on-demand, DVD distribution, broadcast and cable television distribution, and inflight airline distribution. At this time, the topic of having a category for best picture for a streaming platform hasn't surfaced, but Apple TV+ is the first streaming service to garner an Oscar for best picture in 2022 for

CODA (2021). Interestingly, there was no firestorm of controversy when that occurred perhaps because the world was in the midst of the Corona virus. In the 2020-2021 Oscar Season, AMPAS granted leniency to studios because cinemas were closed due to the COVID-19 pandemic.

Be aware this rule will be amended in the future, as AMPAS announced a change in June 2023 regarding screening for best picture hopefuls. Beginning in 2024, studios must expand the screening of their movies to be shown in 10 of the top 50 U.S. markets, no later than 45 days after the initial release in 2024. This is in addition to the foundational requirement of a one-week theatrical release in one of the six U.S. qualifying cities: Los Angeles County, New York, the Bay Area, Atlanta, Chicago, and Miami. A loophole allows international markets to count toward two of the 10 U.S. top markets. According to an AMPAS press release. the purpose of this change for the expanded theatrical footprint to increase the visibility of films worldwide and encourage audiences to experience our artform in a theatrical setting.

Rule 3: The Awards Year and Deadlines

Film companies that want their movie to be considered for an Oscar must have a theatrical qualifying run between January 1 and December 31. This rule is different for animated feature films, documentaries, international feature films, and short films.

AMPAS allows filmmakers to exhibit their movies in theaters in other U.S. cities before their theatrical qualifying run, only if the screening is at a film festival, in a commercial motion picture theater, or as a theatrical preview. If filmmakers show the movie on nontheatrical channels before a theatrical qualifying run, they will become ineligible for an Oscar nomination. Film companies can exhibit their film outside the United States in a commercial theater before a theatrical qualifying run if it's their first exhibition, and they can exhibit on nontheatrical media outside the United States only.

The submission deadline depends upon their qualifying run. For films that have runs within the months of January and June, their submission is due September 15. For films that have runs within the months of July and December, their submission is due November 15. This deadline applies to films for general entry and animated feature category. This is a recent change, as in years past, submissions for all films that were up for Oscar consideration were due mid-December.

There are some categories that have a different due date. They are as follows:

August and October
Animated Short Film
Documentary Feature
Documentary Short Subject
Live Action Short Film

October
International Feature Film

November
Original Score
Original Song
Sound

Rule 4: Submission

Two major topics are covered in this section: the submission of the film with all its promotional materials and the conditions that apply to a film and its creators if they win an Oscar. AMPAS requires a high-quality copy of the film and related marketing materials. If nominated, AMPAS screens the movie for members to view for voting consideration, and it takes excerpts to use for events. Film companies must agree to give AMPAS these materials as part of the submission requirements, and the organization keeps these materials in their archives.

This rule also states the Oscar statuette cannot be disposed of or sold. Unfortunately, this has happened in the past with heirs of Academy Award winners, so AMPAS includes a condition that the recipient of an Oscar can sell it back to AMPAS for $1 if they no longer want possession of it. Having the Academy Award does not give the recipient rights to AMPAS's trademark, copyright, or service mark.

Rule 5: Balloting and Nominations

Active and lifetime members of AMPAS may vote. Voting members do so by secret ballot and those ballots are tabulated by an accounting firm PwC (PricewaterhouseCoopers). Non-voting members of AMPAS are those who are deemed emeritus, and any members who are inactive (not having worked in the movie industry in the last 30 years).

Not mentioned in rule 5 is the preliminary voting and nomination voting process, which occurs prior to nomination determinations. Typically, members of each branch first vote on which films or individuals should be on the ballot just for categories within their respective branches. For example, actors are only selecting people for best performance by an actor and actress in a leading and supporting role. Normally, preliminary voting for every category takes place in December when members only vote for film nominations in their respective category and vote for best picture nominations. AMPAS announces a short list of potential nominees in nine categories: documentary feature, documentary short subject, international feature film, makeup and hairstyling, original score, original song, animated short film, live action short film, and visual effects. The process to finalize nominees differs per AMPAS branch, and short lists are announced in December. Typically, AMPAS voters determine Oscar nominees in January.

All voting members also consider films for the coveted best picture category. In December, AMPAS publishes a Reminder List document that contains all the feature films eligible for an Academy Award. In 2022, 301 feature films were eligible for

Oscars consideration; 276 movies in 2021, were eligible, 366 in 2020, and 344 in 2019. This includes films longer than 40 minutes, including documentary, animation, and international films. It excludes short films.

Rules 6 through 27

Rules 6 through 24 pertain to individual award categories. For example, rule 7 pertains to animated feature films, rule 18 pertains to music categories, and rules 25 and 26 pertain to the Governors Awards, and rule 27 is for scientific and technical special awards. In a general sense, this range of rules serves, among other things, to define film type, establish how many statuettes are distributed, specify eligibility requirements, and outline submission and voting procedures.

Rule 19 Best Picture

This is the highly anticipated game changing rule that is applicable to films released in 2023 and beyond for the foreseeable future has been on the movie industry's forefront since 2021 when AMPAS announced its Representation and Inclusion (RAISE) initiative. This new requirement applies to films in consideration for best picture, which can include animated feature, international feature and documentary feature films if studios want to enter that race.

Interestingly, RAISE requirements are not specified in Rule 19, however they are posted on AMPAS's website. According to AMPAS, RAISE is designed to encourage equitable representation on and off screen to better reflect the diverse global population. This rule change suppports AMPAS's Aperture 2025 initiative, an extension of its prior A2020 campaign for diversity and inclusion meant to remedy Oscars So White criticism.

Here are the details as stated on AMPAS's website dated August 2022, and as of this book's revision June 2023:

For the 96th Oscars (Award Show 2024), submitting a confidential Academy Inclusion Standards form (RAISE) and meeting two out of four of the following standards will be required in order for the film to be deemed eligible:

Standard A: On-screen representation, themes and narratives

A film can achieve this standard by meeting the criteria in at least one of the following areas:

A1. Lead or significant supporting actors from underrepresented racial or ethnic groups

At least one of the lead actors or significant supporting actors is from an underrepresented racial or ethnic group in a specific country or territory of production. This may include:

- African American / Black / African and/or Caribbean descent
- East Asian (including Chinese, Japanese, Korean, and Mongolian)
- Hispanic or Latina/e/o/x
- Indigenous Peoples (including Native American / Alaskan Native)
- Middle Eastern / North African
- Pacific Islander
- South Asian (including Bangladeshi, Bhutanese, Indian, Nepali, Pakistani, and Sri Lankan)
- Southeast Asian (including Burmese, Cambodian, Filipino, Hmong, Indonesian, Laotian, Malaysian, Mien, Singaporean, Thai, and Vietnamese)

A2. General ensemble cast

At least 30% of all actors in secondary and more minor roles are from at least two underrepresented groups, which may include:

- Women
- Racial or ethnic group
- LGBTQ+
- People with cognitive or physical disabilities, or who

are deaf or hard of hearing

A3. Main storyline/subject matter

The main storyline(s), theme or narrative of the film is centered on an underrepresented group(s).

- Women
- Racial or ethnic group
- LGBTQ+
- People with cognitive or physical disabilities, or who are deaf or hard of hearing

Standard B: Creative Leadership and Project Team

A film can achieve this standard by meeting the criteria in at least one of the following areas:

B1. Creative leadership and department heads

At least two of the following creative leadership positions and department heads—Casting Director, Cinematographer, Composer, Costume Designer, Director, Editor, Hairstylist, Makeup Artist, Producer, Production Designer, Set Decorator, Sound, VFX Supervisor, Writer—are from an underrepresented group and at least one of those positions must belong to someone from an underrepresented racial or ethnic group. Underrepresented groups may include:

- Women
- Racial or ethnic group
- LGBTQ+
- People with cognitive or physical disabilities, or who are deaf or hard of hearing

Underrepresented racial or ethnic groups may include:

- African American / Black / African and/or Caribbean descent
- East Asian (including Chinese, Japanese, Korean, and

Mongolian)
- Hispanic or Latina/e/o/x
- Indigenous Peoples (including Native American / Alaskan Native)
- Middle Eastern / North African
- Pacific Islander
- South Asian (including Bangladeshi, Bhutanese, Indian, Nepali, Pakistani, and Sri Lankan)
- Southeast Asian (including Burmese, Cambodian, Filipino, Hmong, Indonesian, Laotian, Malaysian, Mien, Singaporean, Thai, and Vietnamese)

B2. Other key roles

At least six (6) other crew/team and technical positions (excluding Production Assistants) are from an underrepresented racial or ethnic group. These positions include but are not limited to First AD, Gaffer, Script Supervisor, etc.

B3. Overall crew composition

At least 30% of the film's crew is from at least two underrepresented groups, which may include:

- Women
- Racial or ethnic group
- LGBTQ+
- People with cognitive or physical disabilities, or who are deaf or hard of hearing

Standard C: Industry Access and Opportunities

A film can achieve this standard by meeting the criteria in at least one of the following areas:

C1. Paid apprenticeship and internship opportunities

The film's distribution or financing company has paid apprenticeships or internships that are from the following underrepresented groups and satisfy the criteria below:

- Women
- Racial or ethnic group
- LGBTQ+
- People with cognitive or physical disabilities, or who are deaf or hard of hearing

The major studios/distributors are required to have substantive, ongoing paid apprenticeships/internships inclusive of underrepresented groups (must also include racial or ethnic groups) in most of the following departments: production/development, physical production, post-production, music, VFX, acquisitions, business affairs, distribution, marketing and publicity.

The mini-major or independent studios/distributors must have a minimum of two apprentices/interns from the above underrepresented groups (at least one from an underrepresented racial or ethnic group) in at least one of the following departments: production/development, physical production, post-production, music, VFX, acquisitions, business affairs, distribution, marketing and publicity.

C2. Training opportunities and skills development (crew)

The film's production, distribution and/or financing company offers training and/or work opportunities for below-the-line skill development to people from the following underrepresented groups:

- Women
- Racial or ethnic group
- LGBTQ+
- People with cognitive or physical disabilities, or who are deaf or hard of hearing

Standard D: Audience Development

To achieve Standard D, the film must meet the criterion below:

D1. Representation in development, marketing, publicity, and distribution

The studio and/or film company has multiple (more than one) in-house senior executives belonging to at least two underrepresented groups on their creative and development, marketing, publicity, and/or distribution teams. At least one individual must belong to an underrepresented racial or ethnic group. Underrepresented groups may include:

- Women
- Racial or ethnic group
- LGBTQ+
- People with cognitive or physical disabilities, or who are deaf or hard of hearing

Underrepresented racial or ethnic groups may include:

- African American / Black / African and/or Caribbean descent
- East Asian (including Chinese, Japanese, Korean, and Mongolian)
- Hispanic or Latina/e/o/x
- Indigenous Peoples (including Native American / Alaskan Native)
- Middle Eastern / North African
- Pacific Islander
- South Asian (including Bangladeshi, Bhutanese, Indian, Nepali, Pakistani, and Sri Lankan)
- Southeast Asian (including Burmese, Cambodian, Filipino, Hmong, Indonesian, Laotian, Malaysian, Mien, Singaporean, Thai, and Vietnamese)

All categories other than best picture will be held to their current eligibility requirements. Films in the specialty feature categories (animated feature film, documentary feature, international feature film) submitted for best picture/general entry consideration will be prompted to participate in the Representation and Inclusion Standards process.

Since AMPAS's announcement in 2021 about RAISE, it has required filmmakers to acknowledge RAISE through its submission form. For movies released in 2021 and 2022, studios' entry form into the Oscars race included forthcoming best picture RAISE requirements, and studio representatives signed off on that to confidentially confirm their acknowledgement of said future ruling. This tactic is perceived as AMPAS's way of managing change that will greatly affect film production for 2023 movie releases and the types of films that follow.

Moving forward, studios that want their movie to be eligible for a best picture Academy Awards must meet two out of four of the following standards:

Standard A: On-screen representation, themes and narratives
Standard B: Creative Leadership and Project Team
Standard C: Industry Access and Opportunities
Standard D: Audience Development

The talent for these positions exist, as demonstrated by the hundreds of film organizations supporting under-represented groups, however the issue is will studios utilize that talent for film projects rather than going to their typical network of individuals. Hopefully minority talent will be given a shot at working on Oscar-worthy films. The challenge is talent and crew provide not wanting to provide their demographic information, as that information is not required to get a job

As mentioned in rule two, more changes for best picture eligibility are on the horizon. For movies released in 2024, studios must expand the screening of their movies to be shown in 10 of the top 50 U.S. markets, no later than 45 days after the initial release in 2024 if they want their movies to be eligible for best picture consideration. Remember, other genres such as animated feature, documentary feature and international feature typically compete in the best picture race, so this new screening requirement may be problematic for studios, not to mention expensive.

Submission Form

For a film to be considered for an Oscar, an authorized representative for the film must complete an Academy Award online submission form on AMPAS's website. First, user registration is required; then the online form can be completed. The submission is only valid for films that meet the general entry requirements. There is no cost to submit an entry; however, documentation of the film's properties, credits, and screenings is required. The online submission form is only available during the submission period. Filmmakers submitting for the first time may have access to the submission FAQs after AMPAS has approved their new account.

PRECEDING FILM AWARDS

In early winter, movie industry organizations host their award programs and begin passing out prizes for films they believe deserve high honor. This is a big part of phase II of Oscar Season because studios, distributors, analysts, and most industry professionals are monitoring and tallying nominations and awards. The implication is that movies with the most awards have a higher chance of Oscar gold, though history has shown that this isn't always a given.

Still, movies that receive accolades at the following prestigious awards programs (listed in chronological order) are generally good bets for Oscar nominations and wins: the Gotham Awards, SAG Awards, Writers Guild Awards, Golden Globes, Producers Guild Awards, BAFTA Awards, DGA Awards, New York Film Critics Awards, LA Film Critics Awards, National Society of Film

Critics Awards, Critics' Choice Awards, and the AMPAS Governors Awards. The categories of interest are best picture, best actor and actress, supporting actor and actress, and best director.

Gotham Awards

Hosted by the Gotham Film & Media Institute formerly known as Independent Filmmaker Project (IFP), the Gotham Awards occur in November or December in New York City. The IFP consists of independent storytellers who recognize independent films and television series, and the Gotham Awards is usually the first awards ceremony that occurs during Oscar Season. In 2018, *The* and *If Beale Street Could Talk* were competing for IFP's best feature prize, prior to being nominated for an Academy Award. Gotham Award winning films *Nomadland* (2020) and *Everything Everywhere All at Once* (2022) went on to earn a best picture Oscar. The Gotham Awards also recognizes the best screenplay, best actress and actor, and best documentary, and numerous other categories.

Spirit Awards

Film Independent, based in Los Angeles, is a nonprofit organization that champions creative independence in visual storytelling. In November, it announces nominees for best feature, best first-time feature, best screenplay, best first screenplay, and best director. Other categories range from best male and female actors to specialty awards, like truer than fiction. Being independent movies, these films have talent you're familiar with but most cinephiles haven't heard of the movie (yet), and typically the nominations happen before most of the movies hit cinemas nationwide. The Spirit Awards usually take place in February.

Screen Actors Guild (SAG) Awards

Members of the Screen Actors Guild (SAG) are actors and actresses from around the world. The SAG Awards program focuses on performances in motion pictures and television, and members vote for best leading female and male, best supporting female and male, and best cast. The television category includes comedy, drama, and television movie or series, whereas the film category considers all movie genres in a single category. In 2022, all four of SAG's award for major acting category winners also earned an Academy Award for their performance in these 2021 films: Will Smith, leading actor for *King Richard*; Jessica Chastain, leading actress for *The Eyes of Tammy Faye*; Troy Kotsur, supporting actor for *CODA*; and Ariana Debose, supporting actress for *West Side Story*. SAG nominations are announced in December, and the ceremony takes place in January before the Academy Awards.

Writers Guild Awards

Hosted by the Writers Guild of America West and Writers Guild of America East and their affiliated writers organizations, this awards program highlights those who write screenplays—original screenplays, adaptations, and documentaries. It also awards writers for television drama, comedy and new series, radio-TV, audio, and new media, and there are also special awards. In 2020, *Parasite* (2019) screenwriters Bong Joon Ho and Han Jin Won earned the Writers Guild Award and an Academy Award for original screenplay, and in 2018, Jordan Peel did the same with his original screenplay for *Get Out* (2017). The same is true for adaptive screenwriters Sian Heder for *CODA* (2021) and Sarah Polley for *Women Talking* (2022). Nominations are announced in December, and the Writers Guild Awards typically occur in February, before the Academy Awards.

Golden Globes Awards

The Hollywood Foreign Press Association has hosted an awards program since 1944, and they recognize excellence in film and television. Today, there are awards given in 14 film categories, many of which mirror Oscar categories. Some pundits thought that Golden Globe winners were sure-bet Oscar winners, but the Golden Globe voters don't create movies like AMPAS members. In addition, the organization's reputation and creditability has diminished over the past couple of years, so its value too has been minimized somewhat. It's really a toss up as to whether a Golden Globe winner will be an Academy Award recipient. For example, in the best picture category, Golden Globe 2019 winners were *Bohemian Rhapsody* (2018) (drama) and *Green Book* (2018) (comedy/musical). The Academy Award 2019 winner was *Green Book.* Golden Globe winners in 2018 were *Three Billboards Outside Ebbing Missouri* (2017) (drama) and *Lady Bird* (2017) (comedy/musical). The Academy Award 2018 winner was *The Shape of Water* (2017). Golden Globe nominations are generally announced in December, and the awards ceremony happens in early January, before the Academy Awards nominations are announced.

Producers Guild Awards

The Producers Guild Awards may not be on the radar of most Oscars fans because many people outside of the film industry do not realize just how significant that role is. Producers bring all the elements of a film together, and the Producers Guild of America (PGA) recognizes nominees who are at the top of their game. Awards analysts know this and take this merit into serious consideration when making Oscar predictions for best picture, best animated feature, and best documentary. In 2022, *CODA* (2021) and in 2023, *Everything Everywhere All at Once* (2022) won a PGA award and an Academy Award for best picture. The PGA announces nominees in November and awards recipients in mid-January, usually before the Academy Award nominations are announced.

BAFTA Awards

The British Academy of Film and Television Arts (BAFTA) hosts its annual award ceremony in London, England, and many of their nominees also become Oscar nominees. BAFTA membership consists of more than 8,600 individuals working in film, television, and the gaming industry. In 2016, BAFTA recognized *The Revenant* (2015) for best film and *Brooklyn* (2015) for outstanding British film. Both were nominated for an Oscar for best picture, though the Academy Award went to *Spotlight* (2015). The BAFTA Awards include film categories that the Oscars do not have, such as outstanding British film and a casting award. Nominations are announced in early January and the awards ceremony takes place in early February before the Academy Awards.

DGA Awards

The Directors Guild of America (DGA) is made up of 19,000 movie professionals who work in a director capacity for film, television, commercials, and documentaries. Founded in 1938, the organization's original purpose was to protect the creative and economic rights of film directors. Now membership includes directors, assistant directors, unit production managers, associate directors, stage managers, and production associates. The DGA Awards are an important precursor to the Academy Awards. Many pundits believe that films whose directors win DGA awards are likely to win an Oscar for best picture. This pairing rarely happens when AMPAS has preferential voting for its best picture category. The last time there was a match was when Ben Affleck won the 2013 DGA Award for directing *Argo* (2012), and *Argo* went on to win the Oscar for best picture and in 2021 when Chloe Zhao earned the DGA award for *Nomadland* (2020) and the movie went on to earn the Oscar for best picture. The DGAs have been happening for more than 70 years, and in addition to recognizing directors in feature films, they also recognize first-time feature film directors. The DGA nominations are announced in early January, and the awards ceremony takes place in late January.

New York Film Critics Awards

Hosted by the New York Film Critics Circle, this awards program has categories much like the Oscars. Members of the New York Film Critics Circle—film reviewers and critics from newspapers, magazines, and online publications—vote for best picture, director, screenplay, actor, actress, supporting actor, supporting actress, cinematography, foreign language, and animated film. They also have a best first feature award. In 2015, there was a difference of opinion between members of the New York Film Critics Circle and AMPAS members. *Boyhood* (2014) received the NY Critics Award for best picture, and the Academy Award went to *Birdman* (2014). As mentioned previously garnering a film award from an industry organization isn't a guarantee the movie will win an Academy Award. Nominations for the New York Film Critics Awards are typically announced in December, and the awards ceremony occurs in January.

LA Film Critics Awards

The Los Angeles Film Critics Association (LAFCA)—approximately 60 film critics writing for print and digital media in the LA area—recognizes outstanding films and numerous roles in the movie-making process. LAFCA gives awards in the usual categories: best picture, director and actors, as well as awards for best production design, best editing, best cinematography, best music score, and three specialty awards. As mentioned previously, film awards that precede the Oscars identify exceptional movies as nominees. Sometimes, LAFCA nominees end up becoming Academy Award nominees, yet there is no guarantee that LAFCA award winners end up as Oscar winners. In 2017, a LAFCA was given to *The Shape of Water* (2017) for cinematography, and weeks later, it was nominated for an Oscar, however the Academy Award for that category went to *Blade Runner 2049* (2017). Interestingly, the LAFCA announces award winners, not nominees, in December and host the awards ceremony in January.

National Society of Film Critics

This group of approximately 65 members has been awarding honors to top films for more than 50 years. However, instead of holding an awards ceremony, the society meets each January to vote and then tweets the names of winners and runners-up from a specific X (formerly Twitter) handle, @NatSocFilmCrix. Categories include the usual: best picture, actors and actresses, director, screenplay, and cinematography, along with specialty awards. In 2014, the society voted Cate Blanchett as the best actress winner for *Blue Jasmine* (2013), and AMPAS agreed, giving her an Oscar just a few weeks later.

Critics' Choice Awards

The annual Critics' Choice Awards is co-hosted by the Broadcast Film Critics Association (the largest film critics organization in the United States and Canada) and the Broadcast Television Journalists Association (a professional group of journalists who write about television). This awards program recognizes the finest in cinematic and television achievement. It is relatively new to awards season, having hosted only 24 ceremonies. Nominees are usually announced in December, and the awards gala takes place in January, typically before the Academy Award nominations are released.

AMPAS Governors Awards

Most of the other award ceremonies hosted by the above-mentioned organizations include special awards to honor lifetime achievements in motion pictures. The Academy of Motion Picture Arts and Sciences also has a stand-alone event—the Governors Awards—that recognizes individuals for their work in film. Academy members can recommend nominees; however, the Board of Governors has sole authority to select the winners. A formal dinner ceremony takes place, usually in November. Past honorees include Spike Lee, Oprah Winfrey, and Steven Spielberg.

OSCAR SEASON – PHASE III

ACADEMY AWARD NOMINEES SELECTED

CHAPTER 3 – GETTING NOMINATED

By the time AMPAS is ready to announce the Academy Award nominees, you're halfway through Oscar Season. You've had your eye on film festivals that occurred mid-year, recognizing which films made their debuts and which movies are getting a lot of publicity. You're aware of the campaign rules and are able to identify promotional tactics. You've paid attention to AMPAS's announcements regarding potential nominee short lists, and you've taken note of movies winning top prizes at other industry award ceremonies.

PRELIMINARY VOTING

In chapter 2, you learned that Academy Award categories have a multiple deadlines. Some branches have an extra step in their voting process. Referred to as preliminary voting, members of specific branches recommend their picks of Oscar-worthy films and then create a short list of those films. The films on the short list are not yet official nominees—they're simply potential nominees. Preliminary voting happens in December, and the short list is publicly announced before the end of the year to fuel excitement for the films being seriously considered, to garner fan engagement, and to promote the upcoming Academy Awards ceremony. The voting rules are subject to change annually, and below are guidelines for the 96th Academy Awards. Here are the some of the award categories that have an extensive preliminary voting process.

International Feature Film

Formerly known as the foreign language feature film category, preliminary voting occurs when a committee consisting of members of the International Feature Film Branch view eligible submissions and vote by secret ballot. They do this in two rounds when determining the short list of potential nominees and when official nominees are selected.

To determine the short list of potential nominees, the committee views eligible submissions and votes for the films they believe fit the criteria of an Oscar-worthy movie. Eligible Academy Award voters may participate in the preliminary voting of this category too. In 2023, there were 92 films representing six continents for considered. All voters must see a set number of films in order to vote, and votes are made in order of preference for up to 15 movies. All votes are by secret ballot. From there, the fifteen films receiving the highest number of votes advance to the next round of nomination voting. These 15 movies become the short list. For the second round of voting to determine the final five nominees, active and life AMPAS members may participate in the vote only by screening all films on the short list. Preferential voting occurs again, and the five motion pictures receiving the highest number of votes shall become the nominations for final voting for the International Feature Film award. The country is credited with the film's title as a nominee.

To be considered as an international film, the movie must be in a language other than English and have English subtitles, be at least 40 minutes in length, and be produced outside the United States. Animated films and documentaries can be considered. A country may submit only one film to represent it, and required materials include a film synopsis, director's filmography, poster of the film's theatrical release, and more.

Documentary Feature and Documentary Short Subject

All Documentary Branch members are welcomed to participate

in the preliminary voting process to make the short list determination for documentary feature and documentary short films. All voters must see a set number of films in order to vote, and votes are made in order of preference for up to 15 movies for both categories. Thereafter, the short list of 15 films per documentary category are announced.

AMPAS took the documentary feature short list one step further in 2018 by collaborating with cinemas to screen the short list of 15 features nationwide. The Academy's Future of Film Committee led the initiative, and the films were made available at mainstream movie houses in select cities for a three-week period early in January of 2019.

There is a second round of balloting when five films are chosen from the short list to be the official Oscar nominees for these categories. Only branch members who have seen all of the short-listed films may cast preferential votes to determine the final nominees.

Short Films: Animated and Live Action

The Short Films and Feature Animation Branch has a similar approach for selecting nominees for both categories. Selections for the animated short film is limited to members of the short films and animation branch, whereas all lifetime and active AMPAS members can participate in the live action selection process. For both sets of participating screeners, members are required to see a set percentage of all the eligible short films. In the past, this branch invited members of the Directors Branch to participate in preliminary voting of the live action short films, and now that privilege is open to all AMPAS members who opt-in. These categories typically have a high number of eligible movies. In 2022, 400 live action short films were eligible for consideration; a record number. In 2018, 81 animated short films qualified.

From there, the members score the films on a preferential system and cast a secret vote for 15 films for each category. A few years ago, this branch had a different scoring system wherein the screener would utilize a 10-point scale, assigning the highest score for the best work (e.g., 10 for excellent, 8 for good, 7 fair, etc.). After the shortlist is determined, branch members who opt-in to screen and determine the final nominations are required to view all 15 films on the shortlist in order to cast their vote for the five films they want to vote in as Oscar nominees.

Makeup and Hairstyling

Being one of the smallest AMPAS branches, there is a communal approach to the makeup and hairstyling nomination process. First, only members of this branch meet to review the Reminder List of eligible films. The potential candidates, identified as artists in AMPAS rules, is able to submit a portfolio of their work on the film, to include before and after photos. Portfolios are not required but artists are encouraged to submit one. Then they vote by secret ballot utilizing preferential voting for up to 10 films demonstrating excellence in makeup and hairstyling. Thereafter, they recommend hair and makeup artists to the branch's executive committee for short list consideration, based upon each artist's contributions.

To aid the preliminary voting process, this branch requires artists to submit a written explanation of the steps they took to create the makeup applications and hairstyles for the movie characters. The documentation reveals details of each artist's role and his or her specific achievement. This branch also asks that movie producers provide excerpts from the movie (maximum of seven minutes) that showcase the talent of the makeup and hairstyling artists. This is known as a bake-off.

The 10 films selected for the short list are publicly announced. All members of this branch who have seen all of the short-listed films will vote in the order of their preference for up to five movies. The five films receiving the most votes become Academy Award nominees.

Visual Effects

An executive committee for the Visual Effects Branch, made up of a select group of active and lifetime members, participate in the preliminary voting process by reviewing the Reminder List of eligible films. The group meets several times, then individual committee members vote by secret ballot for up to 20 movies they believe demonstrate considerable contributions to the film. From there, the executive committee sees the movies listed and reduces the list to 10 films, which will be publicly announced as potential nominees.

The executive committee requires additional materials from the short-listed films in order to determine the five nominees. Producers of these films are required to submit movie clips showing the visual effects (maximum of 10 minutes in length), visual materials illustrating the procedures used, written descriptions of the procedures used, rosters of the craftspeople responsible for the work, and the percentage of the individual contributions of those craftspeople. This too is bake-off.

Only active and lifetime members of the Visual Effect Branch may vote for the five films they believe are worthy of being an Oscar nominee. This branch uses a reweighted range voting to determine the final five Academy Award nominees for this category. Up to four individuals who were primarily responsible for visuals effects may be named as nominees for each movie.

Original Score and Original Song

Music Branch members see movie clips of all the eligible films for these categories, then vote according to preference. A short list of 15 potential nominees for each category is determined.

To be eligible for these categories, the music must be original and must have been created specifically for the film. Submission packages for original score must include a final music cue sheet listing all music cues, original score, original songs, source music, and a completed music breakdown form. An original song submission package must include a vocal lead sheet, a digital film clip of each song (maximum of three minutes) showing how the song was incorporated in the movie, and an original song contribution sheet. This last item is required to reveal each song writer's contributions and specific percentages of their work. In 2018, there were 156 scores eligible for consideration, and 90 songs were eligible for original song.

The short list for original score is named by movie title and the short list for original song is named by song title and movie title. Another round of preferential voting takes place using both short lists as the only films for consideration, and five films from each category with the highest number of votes are selected to be official Academy Award nominees.

The original song category is interesting because the song placement in the film and the artists selected to sing are very strategic. A song that studios want as an Oscar contender doesn't have to be in the film's plot. It can be played in the movie's credits, at the end of the film, thus meeting the requirements for consideration. For example, U2's "Ordinary Love" nominated for Original Song played in the credits of Mandela: Long Walk to Freedom (2013). Another strategy to earn a nomination is to have a popular artist sing you film's tune. For example, the songs performed by Lady Gaga have earned three different Original Song nominations, one of them for a documentary film.

Another unique fact about the original song category is that it's the only one that has a group award. If there are more than two songwriters who equally contributed to the song's creation, then one Academy Award is given to the group. At submission, each contributor must sign a consent acknowledging this stipulation in the event their song is Oscar-worthy. In some cases when there are three songwriters, a third statuette may be given, as deemed by the Music Branch. In 2022, the average number of songwriters credited on a Billboard Hot 100 No.1 is 6.4, compared with 4.77 in 2009, according to Billboard magazine.

DETERMINING NOMINEES

Every branch has its own process for determining nominees for its respective categories. Steps outlined in the preliminary voting section of this book give examples of AMPAS members' approach to determining a film's merits. Only branch members can determine the nominees for award categories within their branch. For example, only members of the Writers Branch can determine nominees for original screenplay and adapted screenplay.

In addition, active and lifetime AMPAS members select best picture nominees. Individuals select five movies, and the films with the most votes from preliminary voting move on to become Oscar nominees. In 2022, there were 301 feature films on the Reminder List. How many of those movies do you think Academy members saw? This question highlights an issue that is rarely addressed. That is, if members only see films they like, then they'll most likely list just those type of films. Diversity can't pierce through the Oscar veil until members are willing to see other types of movies.

After all the nominees for each award category have been announced, every active and lifetime AMPAS member may vote in all the award categories. Preferential voting is the method used for selecting only the Best Picture film, when individual members rank their choices from one to 10. For the other categories, voters only select one nominee. More information about voting is outlined in chapter 4.

Preliminary voting ends phase II of Oscar Season, and even though there is a select group of AMPAS members who determine the final nominees for their respective categories, all voting members have a say in which film to nominate for best picture. Studios have been promoting throughout the season in hopes their film will make the list. Large film companies hire campaign consultants who charge up to $25,0000 a month and may also negotiate bonuses if films get nominated.

CHAPTER 4 – NOMINEES REVEALED

Phase III of Oscar Season begins when AMPAS reveals films selected as Oscar nominees. By this time, film studios have been marketing Academy Award hopefuls for months, and Academy members know which films have racked up nominations and awards at other film programs. On the day nominations are announced, emotions run high and judgement is rampant as the countdown to Oscar Night begins.

NOMINATIONS ANNOUNCED

For years, nominees are revealed at the end of January on ABC-TV in the morning. Typically, Good Morning America does a live feed from New York City to AMPAS in Beverly Hills, when celebrities announce nominees for the major award categories. In 2019, the announcement was broadcast on social media about an hour before nominees were revealed on television, an activity that continues today.

On this day, AMPAS releases a beautifully formatted PDF containing the complete list of nominees that can be downloaded from oscars.go.com. The list contains nominees for all 23 categories. If there are films that meet the requirements for best musical score, then there will be 24 categories. When reviewing the categories, you'll notice some are elements of filmmaking (cinematography, director, production design) and some are genres (international film, documentaries, short film). All award categories have five nominees, except best picture which has 10.

The best picture award is the most coveted, and in the past the number of nominees has varied from year to year from 5, but no more than 10. Currently ten films make the best picture list. Typically, best picture nominees have also been nominated in other categories. For example, the film's director, lead actor, or screenplay writer(s) may have been nominated within their specialty categories. Some best picture nominees can rack up nominations in the double digits. It's interesting to identify those movies and see how they fared in other award programs that occurred prior to the Oscars.

SNUBS AND FLUBS

Snubs

The Academy Awards is the last movie ceremony of awards season, and preceding award programs have already clued film fans which movies deserve to win. People take those accolades as a cue to get a jump-start on their Oscar viewing before the nominations are even announced.

Of course, film critics, awards analysts, industry professionals, and pundits have their opinions about which films should be nominated. The common denominator between Oscar fans and the industry professionals is that they all have their favorites. Film fans, studio executives, industry professionals and movie cast and crew tune-in nervously hoping that their film will be announced as an Academy Award nominee. They're practically holding their breath, having faith they're on the ballot.

Snubs are inevitable, and the insult is obvious when films have been nominated for and have even won coveted awards at other major ceremonies. It happens every year, and no reasoning or apology is offered, so media and movie fans are left to speculate what went wrong. For example, *Crazy Rich Asians* (2018), one of the highest-grossing movies of the year, did not receive a single Academy Award nomination, even though it racked up nominations at the Golden Globes, Screen Actors Guild, and the PGA Awards, and won awards at dozens of other ceremonies.

What most fans don't know is that studios have been campaigning their films during the pre-nomination phase. What is common knowledge is that, regardless of campaigning stunts, there is no guarantee of a nomination. In late 2018, Netflix promoted *Dumplin* (2018) by putting singer and songwriter Dolly Parton out front and center in the campaign. Alongside Linda Perry, Parton wrote and recorded the song "Girl in the Movies" for the movie, and their campaigning garnered a Golden Globe nomination. Taking a shot at an Oscar nomination, Netflix hosted a lovely luncheon in a Four Seasons Los Angeles ballroom, where Parton performed "Girl in the Movies." Days later, guests received a Christmas ornament in the shape of a pink guitar. Although you can probably guess what Parton's Christmas wish was that year, AMPAS didn't grant it. She got snubbed.

Even past Oscar winners aren't guaranteed a nomination for current work. Tom Hanks, an Oscar-winning actor in *Philadelphia* (1993) and *Forrest Gump* (1994), and an Academy Award nominee for *Cast Away* (2000), was snubbed in 2018 when he wasn't selected as an Oscar nominee for *The Post* (2017). As the leading male actor in *The Post*, he was a Golden Globe nominee and a Critic's Choice nominee. Tom has been in other Oscar-nominated films since then, such as *News of the World* (2020) and *Elvis* (2022) but did not receive a nomination for his acting in those films.

The diversity of nominees, particularly acting and directing remain under scrunity. Even though AMPAS's new RAISE requirements are around the corner, there are mixed reviews as to their effectiveness. In 2023, nominees for Best Supporting Actress were all White, snubbing Angela Bassett in spite of her Golden Globe and Critics Choice win for *Black Panther: Wakanda Forever* (2022). Being that women are considered a minority, other recent snubs included Gina Prince-Bythewoods, director for *The Women King* (2022) and Taylor Swift, songwriter and singer of "Where the Crawdads Sing" from the movie with the same title.

AMPAS wants to know how artists and craftspeople identify as their nationality, sexual orientation and even disabilities and/or diseases/illnesses, most of which is consider private information. When studios and filmmakers complete a submission form to AMPAS, questions about the all talent and crewmembers must be answered to ensure the film meets the eligibility requirements for Oscar consideration. During the soft rollout of RAISE, 2020 -2022, some questions on the submission form were not answered because the submitter(s) did not know the answer and/or were not allowed to ask due to privacy policies.

Unfortunately, snubs happen to the deceased, too. To honor those who have died in the year since the previous Oscar ceremony, the Academy has a slideshow with pictures of the recently departed. But occasionally, remarkable industry professionals are left out of this *in memoriam* slideshow. Some well-known industry professionals who were omitted from the memorial presentation include Carol Channing (Oscar-nominated actress), Glen Campbell (Oscar-nominated music artist), Verne Troyer (the actor who played Mini-Me in "*ustin Powers* films), David Cassidy (actor), Gary Kurtz (producer of *Star Wars* films), and numerous others who were well-known among the film industry.

Flubs

It seems when the spotlight is on the Academy during Oscar Season, it shines a spotlight on their flaws. As pristine, prim, and proper they appear to be on the outside, they have issues like any other organization. For example, 2019 was a triple-flub year for AMPAS: Kevin Hart backed out as host, the proposition for a "Popular Film" category was squashed, and the decision to not air four award categories was reversed. To increase viewership, the Academy likes to hire an emcee that is popular in mainstream media so that the emcee's followers will tune in to the telecast. Ratings had been down for years, and AMPAS thought Kevin Hart was the answer to increasing those numbers. He graciously accepted until AMPAS asked him to apologize for past derogatory Twitter comments he made about homosexuals. He claimed he had addressed the issue in the past and wasn't going to do it again, and he respectfully stepped down as the Oscar host for the 91st Academy Awards.

In the vein of viewership, AMPAS thought having a "Popular Film" award category would be a hit and boost ratings, but that idea didn't last long when it went public. AMPAS claimed that this new category would be an avenue to recognize movies which might not have been considered otherwise. One of the reasons it was a controversial proposal was that it is difficult to define "popular film." Does that mean box office sales? And if so, would that be limited to US ticket sales or worldwide sales? Would it include revenue from streaming and online viewing? Current award guidelines define a film's eligibility for each award category, but none of those guidelines have ever requested revenue figures.

The third major flub in 2019 occurred when the AMPAS president emailed its members to say that four categories—cinematography, film editing, live action short, and makeup and hairstyling—would be awarded during the commercial breaks of the Oscars telecast. The idea was to meet the viewing patterns of today's audience living in multimedia world. Of course, members of those branches were outraged. They protested, and the Board of Governors reversed the decision.

Two years earlier, in 2017, the wrong movie was announced as the best picture winner, which led to a major unveiling of what happens backstage during the ceremony. Faye Dunaway and Warren Beatty were selected as Oscar presenters to commemorate the 50th anniversary of *Bonnie and Clyde* (1967). When the time came to announce the award for best picture, they were given the wrong envelope. PricewaterhouseCoopers (PwC) employees

Brian Cullinan, who was responsible for the security and distribution of the sealed winners envelopes, was too busy taking pictures of newly awarded Oscar winner Emma Stone backstage and posting to social media. Cullinan mistakenly handed Beatty the envelope for best actress in a Leading Role instead of best picture. When Beatty opened the envelope on stage, he read the information to himself and knew something was wrong. Dunaway took the envelope from Beatty, saw *La La Land* and announced *La La Land* (2016) as the best picture. Jordan Horowitz, producer for *La La Land* discovered the error and proclaimed a mistake has occurred and that *Moonlight* (2016) was the actual winner. This shocked the 3,400 people seated inside the Dolby Theatre and the televised audience of approximately 26.5 million viewers. In the days that followed, flaws in AMPAS's process and protocol were revealed, and PwC's culpability was made known. The subject of integrity and work ethic surfaced, and fans were curious to know if PwC still had a role at the Oscars. Some could say Bonnie and Clyde " robbed *Moonlight* of its best picture Academy Award limelight..

Most recently is AMPAS's flub after Will Smith, best actor nominee slapped guest presenter, Chris Rock, comedian at the 94th Academy Awards ceremony in 2022. Many believe that Smith should have been immediately removed from the premises after the assault yet he was allowed to stay, eventually to receive an Oscar for his acting in *King Richard* (2021), giving an acceptance speech, Even after Smith resigned as an AMPAS member a couple of weeks after the incident, it still took AMPAS days thereafter to ban Smith from Oscar ceremonies for the next 10 years and to revoke his membership.

The flub that happens the most often is the mispronunciation of nominees' and winners' names, especially in the international feature film category. The Academy Awards is a filmmaker's moment of glory, and to have his or her name butchered, even unintentionally, is insulting. Ironically, it is usually an actor or actress who flubs it up. They could easily have been coached on the correct pronunciation and rehearsed. Consider what happened in 2014 when John Travolta, himself an Oscar nominee, mangled famed American singer Idina Menzel's name. She was about to take the stage to sing "Let It Go" from the movie *Frozen* (2013), and he introduced her as Adele Dazeem. That led to a lot of criticism and a public apology from Travolta. At the Oscars the following year, Menzel brought Travolta's flub back to attention by purposely using the made-up name Glom Gazingo to introduce Travolta to the stage.

Some flubs are more serious and have a lasting effect on individual members, the movie industry, and its fan base. The predominately White organization received public criticism in 2015 for having only white nominees in the acting categories. The hashtag #OscarsSoWhite brought media attention to the issue that the Academy Award nominees lacked diversity. The outcry sparked talks of boycotting and getting civil rights organizations involved. In January 2016, AMPAS announced it was committed to doubling the number of women and minority members by 2020, a campaign referred to as A2020. It added three new positions to the Board of Governors, with the caveat that the AMPAS president would personally make the recommendations for people to fill those roles. The organization also decided to place new members in leadership roles on its executive and board committees. Lastly, it increased the number of new member invitations: 322 people in 2015 and 683 in 2016. In 2019, 842 individuals were invited to join AMPAS. In recent years, due to leadership changes, the number of invitees has diminished, but the intention to diversify is still there. In 2023, AMPAS invited 398 artists and professionals to join the organization, and reported of the 2023 class, 40 percent identify as women, 34 percent belong to underrepresented ethnic/racial communities, and 52 percent are from 50 countries and territories outside the United States.

The #MeToo movement and #TimesUp movement were sparked when Harvey Weinstein, a former AMPAS member and

Oscar-winning producer for best picture film *Shakespeare in Love* (1998), was accused of sexual assault and rape. After the *New York Times* broke the story in October 2017, women from all around the United States came forward, mostly on social media, to share their experience of uninvited sexual advances and pressure to perform on the casting couch. Weinstein was expelled from AMPAS and the organization implemented a behavior policy for members. Its Standards of Conduct was released in December 2017, and its first policy addressed sexual harassment. Soon thereafter, Bill Cosby and Roman Polanski were expelled as well.

All through its history, AMPAS has been slow to react when it comes to damage control. It seems like AMPAS's Board of Governors has to convene on public issues before an official statement is made. The Board currently consists of 63 people, so the task of scheduling a meeting is like moving a mountain. There are three members to represent 17 branches; they are designated as Governors. The AMPAS president also assigns three others to the Board as Governors-At-Large. At a time when messages spread like wildfire on social media and mainstream media, AMPAS's slow response to issues may become an increasingly significant liability.

CAMPAIGNING

In addition to the spotlight shining on AMPAS soon after the snubs and flubs have been revealed, film studios are trying to cast a brighter light on their films. Now that they have an official Academy Award nominee on their hands, their promotional engine is put into high gear. The more nominations, the harder the push. Similar to a political campaign, representatives such as actors, actresses, producers, directors, and studio executives are shaking hands, attending events, participating in panel discussions, and more. Their target audience is slightly different than before preliminary voting because they now want to influence all 9,500+ voting AMPAS members rather than merely the members in a film's respective category.

Some studios have been known to spend as much as $30 million to campaign for nominees during Oscar Season. According to *The Hollywood Reporter*, larger studios, like Amazon and Netflix, can afford to spend in the double-digit millions, whereas smaller studios, like Focus Features have a smaller budget around $5–10 million.

Studios are supposed to promote within the rules (see chapter 1 for campaign guidelines), but they come up with unique ways to work around those restrictions in an effort to sway AMPAS voters to love their film. For example, Netflix organized an exhibit showing photography of the production sets for *Roma* (2018) as well as a costume exhibit. In addition, AMAPS voters received a coffee table book containing photographs from the film and a large black pillow with letters that spelled the film's title in bright yellow.

Taking it a little further, some studios use the film's characters as an avenue to make an impact on voting members. When *Vice* (2018) was under consideration, Annapurna Pictures gifted voters with a digital heart rate monitor to acknowledge the film's main character, Dick Cheney, who had heart issues. To promote *First Reformed* (2017), the studio A24 gave voters a bottle of whiskey and Pepto Bismol, the favorite concoction of the main character Toller, played by Ethan Hawke.

Studios hire public relations agencies that specialize in this type of promotion to work their magic close to preliminary voting. Some film companies agree to pay these professional campaign strategists a bonus if a film gets an Oscar nomination. Their job is to come up with ways to get voting members to see a film, connect with it, and vote for it.

Public relations agencies are by no means the only expense a studio might incur in its quest to secure an Oscar nomination. A lot of the time, A-list actors and actresses from the films are out on the campaign trail promoting movies, too—a task they don't do for free. Film festivals are mainly in the United States and Europe, whereas awards programs are mainly in Los Angeles and New York City. For talent to attend these events, costs include wardrobe, hairstyling, makeup, luxury hotels or housing, first-class airline transportation or private jet, black car transportation service, extravagant meals, and of course, the cost for their time and attention.

Although AMPAS members are located worldwide, campaigning is most evident in the Los Angeles area where a majority of members live. Nominated films are on billboards, and movie posters of nominees are at bus stops across town. There are TV ads promoting movies on major networks, and being that most campaigning occurs during the holiday season, DVDs of movies and other gift items become available. There are also full-page ads in industry print magazines and stories to consumer publications featuring the inside scoop of nominated films and the talent in those productions.

CHAPTER 5 – SELECTING OSCAR WINNERS

When the Academy Award nominees are announced, the films that didn't make the cut stop campaigning, and the movies that are on the ballot kick it up a few notches. AMPAS isn't policing campaign activity 24/7; it trusts studios will play by the rules while trying to influence members to vote for their film. For voting to be authentic, AMPAS members should see all the nominees to make an informed decision before completing their ballot. Film companies and AMPAS provide opportunities for members to see nominated films, with some of them preferring a cinema versus a digital (streaming) experience. Re-releasing films is a money maker for studios, too, because movie fans will pay to see nominated films.

AMPAS'S VIEWING PREFERENCE

Many movie fans wonder why commercial films, which are obviously well received based on ticket sales and extended screening periods, aren't usually nominated for an Academy Award. In some cases, nominated films are movies that the general public in the United States isn't interested in seeing. Sometimes the general public has not even heard of some nominees. Film critics and awards analysts believe AMPAS members are partial to art films over commercial films, as has been evident by their nominee selections over the years. AMPAS has waivered its stance on the best picture category over the years, and it highly likely to change in the future.

To try to remedy the disparity between art films and commercial movies, AMPAS has changed the number of best picture nominees a couple of times within the last decade. Five was the magic number of nominees the Academy has had in place since 1944. In 2009, the organization increased best picture nominees to 10 films—a change that was prompted when the highly popular comic book adaptation *The Dark Knight* (2008) was snubbed. The idea for increasing the best picture nominees was to give room for popular films to enter the race. Some Academy members complained that having too many nominees diluted the merit, while others were pleased with the opportunity to get their film in. Some of the popular films of 2009 that were nominated included *Avatar* and *Up*, an animated film. On the flip side, commercial movies that were snubbed that year included *The Hangover* and *Star Trek*.

AMPAS reevaluated the situation in 2011 and decided to change the nominee slots to at least 5 and no more than 10 movies for best picture. This helped maintain the integrity of the award, allowing high-scoring films to rise to the top while omitting lower-scoring films from the list of potential nominees, after the preliminary voting concludes. No sense in padding the best picture nominee list with more than five movies if other films earn little recognition from AMPAS voters in the preliminary round.

Then in 2020 and 2021, AMPAS turned the tables again, and decided on a firm number 10. Rules were updated to state that a set number of ten films will be named as best picture nominees, starting with movies released in 2021. More layers of complexity have been added for future Oscar Seasons, as stated earlier, so it will be interesting to see if AMPAS members will still prefer art films over commercial films, as demonstrated by the organization's nomination patterns since the best picture rule has changed a few times. Admittedly, commercial films—even animated features—have made it as nominees; however, the art films still outnumber them.

At the 91st Academy Awards in February 2019, three blockbuster films released in 2018 had a shot at the best picture Academy Award: *Black Panther*, *Bohemian Rhapsody*, and *A Star Is Born*. Finally, films that were popular among mainstream movie-goers were recognized for their film excellence. It had been two decades since this phenomenon occurred; *Titanic* (1997) was the last high-grossing popular film to earn the distinction of best picture nominee and winner. According to IMDB.com, *Titanic* was the highest-grossing film in 1997, earning $659.33 million. To give you some perspective, *Men in Black* came in second, grossing $250.69 million.

It looked like AMPAS was making progress, having selected *Black Panther*, *Bohemian Rhapsody*, and *A Star Is Born* as best picture nominees. According to IMDB.com, *Black Panther* was the highest-grossing film in 2018, earning $700.06 million. *Bohemian Rhapsody* was 10th with $216.43 million, and *A Star Is Born* was 11th, earning $215.29 million. It's obvious AMPAS members thought highly of these films' artistic and scientific merit; however, voters believed *Green Book* (2018), which ranked 36th on IMDB's list, was more deserving of the best picture Academy Award. History was made in 2020, at the 92nd Academy Awards when *Parasite*, a non-English language film from South Korea won best picture; the first time ever, an international film has received a best picture award. Not only that, *Parasite* also made history by being the only foreign language film to earn the award for best original screenplay, best director, and best picture.

PREFERENTIAL VOTING

Active and lifetime members of AMPAS have the honor of voting for one film in each of the individual 23 categories. When you add together the total run-time for all nominated films, you'll see that members must invest days upon days of viewing. To do it right, members should evaluate films based upon the categories each film is nominated for. For example, if the movie is nominated for cinematography and screenwriting, then viewers should pay attention to the camera shots and story.

When it's time for AMPAS members to make their final selections, they cast their ballots online. The assumption is that each voter has seen all of the nominees and is making selections based upon a film's excellence in motion picture art and science and upon a sincere belief that the film is the best in the category for which it was nominated.

The best picture category is the only one in which voters select films in preference order, such as their first choice winner, second choice winner and so on. According to AMPAS, a preferential balloting method is the best way to determine which film is most liked by its approximately 9,500+ voting members. This is a different approach than tallying the film that got the most votes. The requirement for determining a winner is for one nominee to receive more than 50 percent of the votes; however, it's highly unlikely that such a result would occur using a popular voting method, since 10 films are on the ballot. Using the preferential balloting means a voter's first choice might not get the majority vote; hence, their second choice is considered.

Envision the process like this. There are 10 best picture nominees, and voters put their preferences for winners on a ballot, giving each film a rank between 1 (the best) and 10 (the least liked). The accounting firm PwC compiles the ballots according to first-choice films. The film that has the least first-choice votes is then eliminated as a contender, and PwC looks at the second-choice markings listed on those ballots and stacks them with that film's first-choice votes. After that, the film that now has the least number of ballots is eliminated as a contender. PwC then looks at the third-choice marks listed on those ballots and stacks them with that film's other ballots. This strike and stack process continues until one film has more than 50 percent of all the ballots. This is how some voters' second, third, or fourth choice can win best picture.

The preferential ballot has shaken up the director-best movie grouping that industry professionals have come to expect. It used to be that when a director won an Academy Award, then his or her film would also win the best picture Oscar. That combo doesn't happen anymore. And no matter how much you analyze wins from other award ceremonies, like the PGA award, BAFTA, or Golden Globes, the Academy Awards best picture winner is still a toss up. In 2022, *CODA* (2021) won best picture and best director went to Jane Campion for *Power of the Dog* (2021). In 2019, *Green Book* won best picture, and Alfonso Cuaron of Roma won best director. In 2018, Spotlight won best picture, and Alejandro G. Inarritu won best director for *The Revenant.* In 2017, *Moonlight* won best picture, and Damien Chazelle won best director for *La La Land.* In short, to predict the best picture winner, you may have to consider which movie is the second or third most deserving film.

All the other categories use the popular voting method. The AMPAS voter selects only one of the five nominees for the other 23 categories, such as production design, sound editing, visual effects, and so on. Votes are cast anonymously, and PwC tallies the votes to determine the Academy Award winner. If voters have not seen all the films in a particular category, they can still vote for one film in that category, or they can abstain.

From the time nominations are announced to when final voting closes, AMPAS voters have approximately four weeks to see all the nominated films. Due to the buzz from film festivals, many members have seen a lot of the nominated films already. In addition, a great number of members belong to industry specific organizations, such as the Screen Actors Guild, the Producers Guild of America, and those groups host awards contests, too. Many of their finalists become Oscar-nominated films, so it is expected that by the time the Academy Award nominations are announced, members have already seen a majority of the films.

Since AMPAS's mission is to recognize and uphold excellence in the motion picture arts and sciences, some members believe nominated films should be viewed in a theater to uphold the standard of excellence. How can one properly evaluate and judge a motion picture if it is viewed on a digital device (monitor, tablet, phone)? Other members prefer the convenience of digital, so they can view at home or elsewhere. There are pros and cons to both viewing methods, but the important thing is for voters to see the films, start to finish, uninterrupted.

VOTER BIAS AND VOTING BODY

According to an article in the February 27, 2016, issue of *The Hollywood Reporter*, AMPAS members shared how they viewed the 2015 best picture nominees. These averaged responses are as follows.

- 5.5% didn't see them
- 18% watched them in a screening room
- 20.5% watched in a regular theater
- 56% watched screeners

At that time, a majority of the screeners were DVDs provided to voters, whereas now, AMPAS has an online digital platform. The same article also revealed that only 4 percent of voters returned or destroyed the screeners after viewing, as instructed. Studios ask viewers to do this so that the screeners (on DVD) are not kept, sold, or gifted. The single digit percentage implies that very few people follow the destruction or return instructions. If an Academy member is caught sharing the screeners, he or she can be suspended or expelled from AMPAS. Thus far in its history, only one member has been expelled for sharing screeners: Carmine Caridi, the actor who played Albert Volpe in *The Godfather: Part II* (1974) and The Godfather: Part III(1990).

The voting body is evolving from mainly being senior-aged White males to being a more diverse demographic. AMPAS reports the diversity facts for incoming members but not as a whole. Back in 2012, an *LA Times* study revealed 94 percent of

AMPAS voters were white, and 77 percent were male. In 2016, the *LA Times* took another look and discovered AMPAS membership was 91 percent white and 75 percent male. To diversity membership, former AMPAS president Cheryl Boone Isaacs spearheaded changes regarding voting privileges, leadership appointments, and new membership offers. In 2020, AMPAS launched its Aperture 2025 initiative, designed to encourage equitable representation on and off screen; changing best picture eligibility requirements.

AMPAS voters are members who are active and lifetime members. A new member has voting privileges for 10 years, and that privilege is renewable if the member remains active in film during that decade. Members achieve lifetime voting privileges after three 10-year terms or if they have been nominated for or have won an Academy Award. Members who do not meet those requirements remain as emeritus members. Emeritus members are still a part of the organization but do not vote.

Incoming members are changing the demographics of the organization, and their preferences for films and platforms differ from their predecessors. Back in the day, voting members were loyal to studios and were known to vote for films from film companies that employed them. Those members spent their careers crafting films for audiences to see in the cinema and stayed true to genres and story structure. New members experience film differently and prefer a streaming experience; they are more open to movies that break the traditional mold. So even though the Academy has a single voting body, there are two distinct groups within it.

When making their final choices, AMPAS voters are supposed to select films based on excellence in motion picture art and science, but they don't always adhere to that guideline. Voter biases have been revealed in interviews *The Hollywood Reporter* has conducted with voters. The magazine's "My Brutally Honest Oscar Ballot" articles relay which branch an anonymous voter is a member of, and which nominee that AMPAS member voted for and why. The voters' identities are not revealed, giving them anonymity to speak freely about their selections. The articles are edited transcripts of conversations with Academy members, which are candid, unfiltered, and unapologetic.

Some brutally honest AMPAS members go into detail about their preferences. For some, it was a process of elimination: they ruled out the movies they didn't like in a particular category, then contemplated and analyzed the remaining films they liked. Some of the reasons they disliked films were they didn't think the characters were believable, the story had holes, the camera angles were dizzying, and so on. Voters also revealed that they based their selections on relationships, active or distant. For example, a member said she voted for a particular actress because the actress had been previously nominated years ago and didn't win an Oscar then, so the actress should be rewarded now. This prejudice works conversely; if a nominee has, in the voter's opinion, earned too many Academy Awards, then the voter would not select that nominee, in hopes of giving another person a chance to win.

When it comes to the genre categories, like international feature film and documentary feature, some voters interviewed revealed they didn't see all the films in those categories yet based their decision on what they did view. Voters usually see international feature films and documentary features on AMPAS's digital platform, and forgo AMPAS's screenings in theaters. Being that these movies are full-length, voters may put them at the bottom of their viewing list and run out of time to see them. These categories are where voters are most likely to abstain.

There were two craft categories that are somewhat of a mystery to voters are the sound editing and sound mixing. Some of the voters who were interviewed for "My Brutally Honest Oscar Ballot" claimed they were unclear about what constitutes excellence in sound editing and sound mixing. They also were unsure about the difference between the two. Coincidentally in 2020, AMPAS combined those two categories into one, called best achievement in sound.

Some voters commented about sexism among nominees. It's typical for men to be named in the directors, cinematographers, and screenwriters categories. Male producers also dominate the best picture category, so when a woman is named in any of those, AMPAS members take notice. Female nominees are usually in the "below-the-line" categories, such as costume design, production design, makeup and hair styling, live-action short films, and animated short films. Women have been successful at directing documentary features and short films which have received Oscar nominations, and of course, there are always the leading and supporting actress categories. Although 2019 was a monumental year when women in the film industry were nominated (59 out of 212 nominees), there should be greater equality in all the categories, particularly those "above-the-line."

CHAPTER 6 – EXCITEMENT BUILDS

There is a string of AMPAS events and activities that lead up to Oscar Night. The Academy hosts other award ceremonies during Oscar Season, and it makes major announcements to reveal the emcee, presenters, and performers appearing at the Academy Awards. At this point, the Academy is increasingly rolling out Oscar-related news and information to get movie fans interested in watching the Academy Awards. Excitement builds as the weeks leading to the Academy Awards decrease.

OTHER AMPAS AWARDS

Most Oscar fans haven't heard of these award ceremonies because they are not as star-studded as the Academy Awards and because they focus more on contributions to the craft rather than on celebrity recognition and fashion.

Governors Awards

This invitation-only, black-tie dinner occurs in the fall when movie industry professionals—most of whom have achieved significant milestones in a lifelong career—are recognized for their work and are awarded an Oscar statuette. Academy members recommend honorees; however, the Board of Governors has sole authority to select winners. Selection typically occurs in September, and the honorees are announced thereafter. The awards ceremony typically takes place in November. The

Governors Awards are the first in a lineup of Academy Awards-specific events that occur during Oscar Season.

There are three different types of awards, though not every type is awarded every year.

The Honorary Award

An Oscar statuette is given to an individual from any traditional discipline in the film industry who has performed exceptional work in his or her lifetime, or to an Academy member who has given outstanding service to the organization, or to a professional who has contributed greatly to the motion picture arts and sciences. Formerly known as the Special Award when inducted in 1929, some recipients are Charlie Chaplin, D.W. Griffith, Fred Astaire, Greta Garbo, Orson Welles, Sophia Loren, and Spike Lee.

The Jean Hersholt Humanitarian Award

Periodically, an Oscar statuette is given to an individual in the motion picture industry whose humanitarian work has made a significant difference in the world. It's appropriately named after Jean Hersholt (1886–1956), a Danish American screen actor in the 1920s who led the Motion Picture Relief Fund as president in the 1930s and '40s. The Motion Picture Relief Fund was an organization that offered financial support to actors and other movie professionals who were out of work or fell on hard times. Hersholt also served as AMPAS president from 1945 to 1949. Some recipients since its 1957 induction include Bob Hope, Frank Sinatra, Audrey Hepburn, Quincy Jones, Jerry Lewis, Oprah Winfrey, and Angelina Jolie.

The Irving G. Thalberg Memorial Award

Specifically recognizing producers whose work has been consistently exceptional and high quality, this award is not an Oscar statuette but rather a gold sculpture of Irving G. Thalberg's head. Thalberg helped form Metro-Goldwyn-Mayer and worked as head of production at age 26, in 1925. He set the standard for outstanding and elegant motion pictures, building a stellar reputation for MGM as an industry leader. This award is also gifted periodically. Some recipients since its 1938 induction are Walt Disney, Cecil B. DeMille, Alfred Hitchcock, Steven Spielberg, George Lucas, and Francis Ford Coppola.

Sci-Tech Awards

AMPAS hosts the Academy's Scientific and Technical Awards at a formal affair in an elegant hotel in the Los Angeles area to honor individuals and corporations that have significantly elevated the use of science and technology in filmmaking. Recognizing early on that science and technology are foundational to movie making, the Academy began acknowledging these industry professionals in 1931 at the fourth Academy Awards. There are three levels of awards: Academy Award of Merit (Class I) winners receive an Oscar statuette, Scientific and Engineering Award (Class II) winners receive a bronze tablet, and Technical Achievement Award (Class III) winners receive a certificate.

John A. Bonner Medal of Commendation

Selected by the Scientific and Technical Awards Committee and the Academy Board of Governors, this honor is awarded to an Academy member who has demonstrated exceptional service and dedication to AMPAS. John A. Bonner, a sound engineer, was Director of Special Projects at Warner Hollywood Studios and had been awarded the Medal of Commendation in 1994. This award is presented at the Sci-Tech Awards ceremony.

Gordon E. Sawyer Award

Given to an individual whose contributions brought credit to the motion picture industry, this honoree is also selected by the Scientific and Technical Awards Committee and the Academy Board of Governors. Named after three-time Oscar winner and former head of the sound department at Samuel Goldwyn

Studios, Gordon E. Sawyer award winners receive an Oscar statuette. This award is presented at the Sci-Tech Awards ceremony.

For decades, the Scientific and Technical Awards took place approximately two weeks before the Oscars; however circumstances have prevented this awards program to maintain a consistent recurring date for the ceremony.

OSCAR NOMINEE LUNCHEON

A few weeks before the Oscar ceremony, all the nominees gather at the Beverly Hilton Hotel for an elegant luncheon hosted by AMPAS. This event, holding a tradition of 38 years and counting, is the Academy's way of welcoming the class of nominees by officially acknowledging their career milestone with a certificate of nomination, relaying the ground rules for acceptance speeches and capturing a group picture for its archive.

This event isn't widely promoted because only nominees and one companion are invited. It's meant to be simple, elegant, and private yet casual so that nominees feel free to mix and mingle without cameras capturing their every move. Being an AMPAS member doesn't guarantee an invitation unless you're on the Board of Governors or a past president. The only non-nominees AMPAS invites are ABC-TV personnel, which broadcasts the Oscars, and select members of the media. A picture of the class is posted on the AMPAS social media.

OSCAR WEEK

Unbeknownst to most fans outside of the Hollywood Hills, there is a special, almost-secret event that precedes Tinsel Town's biggest night of the year: Oscar Week. It's a series of public programs in the days that precede the Oscars in which filmmakers participate in panel discussions about their films that have been nominated for an Academy Award. The week has five or six individual events, each dedicated to a specific Oscar award category.

The purpose of Oscar Week is to celebrate select categories of nominated films, but it's more than that. You are in the same room with Oscar nominees, and hearing their stories of trials and triumphs during the filmmaking process is both thrilling and inspiring. It makes you feel connected to the filmmakers and their movies on a deeper level.

Most of the films honored during Oscar Week are not typical mainstream movies. The select categories are:

Short Films: Animated and Live Action
Documentaries: Short and Feature
Animated Features
International Features
Makeup and Hairstyling

On occasion, there is an Oscar Concert. This musical event seldom occurs, and although it's part of Oscar Week, it's not promoted with the other events when it does happen.

Diehard fans who want an authentic Oscar experience need to read "Experience Oscar Week: Get in on Academy Award Action," a companion to this book. It's the only event guide that relays details about this unique Oscar event and why it's a must for filmmakers and Academy Awards fans. That book also gives details about attending AMPAS's only public Oscar Night at the Museum party that is a must-do for Academy Award fans.

STARS ANNOUNCED

One of the biggest draws for movie fans to watch the Oscars is seeing their favorite celebrities present or perform. Knowing popular film actors and actresses have a large following, AMPAS books them to be on stage at the Academy Awards to introduce a category of nominees or to introduce a musical guest.

A couple of weeks after the Academy Award nominations are announced, AMPAS begins to reveal who will be at the Oscars.

The caliber of talent invited to be a part of the production ranges from actors who play superheroes to previous Oscar winners. Decades ago, AMPAS seemed to fulfill this role with members only. It was very common that presenters were the previous year's award winners. They would announce the current nominees for a category, and then proclaim the winner for that category. In recent years, however, presenters have been SNL alumni, James Bond 007 actors, and pop singers who work in the film industry.

The 2019, AMPAS went beyond TV and film stars to include world-renowned tennis champion Serena Williams and Congressman John Lewis (D-Ga) as presenters. Interestingly, some celebrities in other industries were in attendance but only showcased on the red carpet, such as country music artist Kacey Musgraves, comedian Sebastian Maniscalco, and YouTube sensation and organizational guru Marie Kondo. On the surface, it looks like a successful attempt to diversify star power.

You can always count on the best original song nominees to be performed at the ceremony. AMPAS rolls out announcements about performances to build excitement. Most of the time the original artist sings; however, there have been occasions when someone else performs. These musical artists are also an attractor factor, so the Academy is sure to get the word out.

Are you wondering why there is no mention of the Academy Awards host? All the details about this critical role are in chapter 7.

OSCAR SEASON – THE BIG REVEAL

ACADEMY AWARDS ACTIVITIES

CHAPTER 7 – OSCAR NIGHT

The Academy Awards event finally happens approximately eight months after Oscar Season launches. This fan guide has informed you about phases I and II of Oscar Season, and now you're at the end of phase III. So much has happened since the season began, and you're now more informed about the journey that filmmakers, studios, and talent take to be included in the most prestigious movie awards ceremony in the world.

THE HOST

This role is a blessing and a curse. The lucky person who is brave enough to accept AMPAS's invitation to emcee the biggest movie awards event of the year has to tap into their super powers—nerves of steel, concrete confidence, and supersonic wit—to pull off a successful three-hour show that is televised live in more than 225 countries and territories worldwide. It's an honor very few in the entertainment industry have received, and it's usually the first to be judged when the ceremony has ended.

Although the hosts for the past nine decades have brought their own styles to the stage, the common denominator is that they're entertaining yet unpredictable. The Academy Awards is a contest, and there will be more losers than winners that night, so the host must find ways to take the edge off this competition. Although the format for the ceremony has pretty much remained the same over the years—announce the winner after all the nominees have been named—the action that happens in between is where the host works his or her magic. The host has to be an exceptionally creative and comedic commentator without being offensive or political.

In 1953, when the Oscars were first televised, Bob Hope, actor and comedian, and Conrad Nagel, actor and Academy Honorary Award recipient, served as co-hosts. Hope was a standout emcee because of his quick wit and humor. Thereafter, Hope took the role more than a dozen times. He was naturally relatable and was nimble with clever commentary throughout the awards program. AMPAS struck gold when they booked Hope as host because he was an expert at setting a jubilant tone from the show's beginning and carrying a light-hearted mood throughout the ceremony while incorporating bits of comedy to keep it entertaining. He established a baseline for how a host should perform and engage, and he met AMPAS's and the television network's expectations for this role. Thus far in Academy Awards' history, Hope holds the record for hosting the most Oscar ceremonies: 19. He was truly a master of ceremonies.

The most prominent Hope successor is Billy Crystal. Comedian-turned-actor, Crystal fit the mold—creative and comedic—and he raised the bar higher by transforming the opening number of the awards ceremony into a must-see showcase. Crystal incorporated song, dance, and costumes to produce musical numbers that audiences looked forward to seeing. Being the host for a film-based awards program, he had videos of movie montages where he would dress up like movie characters and act out a scene with an added twist. Some montages focused on nominated films and some montages were compilations of notorious films, such as *The Godfather* (1972) and *The Exorcist* (1973). Crystal would place himself in the movie scenes, either as a character from the film or in a role that he made up for a film scene, costume and all. Crystal was the kind of host who had you guessing about his opening number. You didn't know what kind of performance he was going to pull off, but you knew it would spectacular, hilarious, and exceptionally entertaining. Audiences happily tuned in to see what he had up his sleeve. In the nine ceremonies he hosted, Crystal demonstrated with great enthusiasm how motion picture arts and science should be celebrated.

Johnny Carson (original host of The Tonight Show on NBC-TV) ranks third in the list of repeat Academy Awards hosts, with five appearances. Carson did a phenomenal job of shaving off layers of intensity with playful one-liners that poked fun at the show's elements, such as its length, the secrecy of the winners, and what happens to the losers after the show. Being a master of the monologue, he started the show with a standup comedy act, and his humor won over thousands of highbrows in the theatre and the millions watching on television. Carson is a special part of Academy Awards history.

Since Billy Crystal's appearances ceased, it seems as though AMPAS has been unable to book a good host for more than a couple of times. Whoopi Goldberg, comedian, actress and TV talkshow host has hosted four times. Jimmy Kimmel, who has hosted three times, will always be remembered as the host during the 2017 best picture envelope mix-up known as envelopegate. A threesome hosted in 2022, with Wanda Sykes, Regina Hall and the witty, Amy Schumer who said "there is a different vibe in here" after Will Smith slapped Chris Rock. Ellen DeGeneres, a two-time host, made her mark when she took a selfie with nominees during the Academy Awards ceremony in 2014, then posted it to Twitter. Other celebrities in the two-time club include Jon Stewart, Chris Rock, and Hugh Jackman.

The Academy promotes the host's role to draw viewership, however, the attention garnered may not be positive, as was the case in 2018 when film and comedy star Kevin Hart accepted and then declined the job. When Hart refused to comply with AMPAS's demands, he stepped down. Instead of replacing Hart, AMPAS decided to go without an emcee. The situation brought light to the fact this wasn't the first time the Academy Awards has gone on without a host. In 1989, the Oscars were hostless, and the ceremony opened with a song and dance by Rob Lowe and Snow White. The ceremony was hostless in 2020 and 2021 too. Additionally, Hart is not the first person to accept and then exit. In 2011, Eddie Murphy, comedian and film star, took the host assignment then quit because the show's producer, Brett Ratner, a colleague of Murphy's, quit under pressure from AMPAS for derogatory comments he made during pre-production.

It's no secret that the Academy wants to expand its audience, particularly among people age 18–49, so they invite celebrities who appeal to that demographic to emcee the show. Celebrities that fit that bill have included Neil Patrick Harris, Seth MacFarlane, Anne Hathaway, James Franco, and others. If you missed seeing these hosts perform at the Oscars, there are video clips of their appearances on the Academy Awards "Oscar" YouTube channel.

There have been numerous other hosts over the years, and the format has evolved. The first (and shortest) Academy Awards ceremony (1927) lasted only 15 minutes and was hosted by founding member, Douglas Fairbanks. Nowadays, although AMPAS may have a list of great candidates, their prospects may not be all that interested. As mentioned earlier, feedback about the host's performance is critiqued immediately, sometimes before the ceremony is even over. Each host wants to bring his or her own creative touch to the ceremony to change things up, but the artistic moves aren't always well received (e.g., Seth McFarlane sang "We Saw Your Boobs," Neil Patrick Harris performed magic tricks, and James Franco dressed in drag). The job begins weeks before Oscar Night, and typically the host works with the script-writing team and producers to prep for the show. The host also commits to publicity activities, including posing for a huge vertical billboard that's placed at the corner of Hollywood Boulevard and Highlands Avenue, just outside the Dolby Theatre. It's a major commitment, having to write the show's script, rehearse and perform, and the pay is mediocre. Jimmy Kimmel revealed he was paid $15,000 to host.

THE RED CARPET

The most popular portion of the Academy Awards is when celebrities and popular personalities strut their stuff on the red carpet. Ladies flaunt their fashion down the crimson road and male attendees peacock on the red runway, too. Feeling like royalty in the finest formal apparel, Oscar nominees, studio executives, members of the AMPAS Board of Directors, and special guests proudly take a walk of fame while posing for hundreds of photographs along the sidelines.

To set the scene, know that the red carpet is more than a single fabric strip of walkway that is outlined with velvet stanchions. The road directly in front of the Dolby Theatre, Hollywood Boulevard, is completely closed off for approximately two weeks before the big night to construct this performance area. Bleacher seats for screaming fans are erected, an enormous curtain is hung from the main exterior archway, and rolls and rolls of red carpet (approximately 16,000 square feet) are secured over several vehicular lanes. There are other functional areas throughout the red carpet that typically aren't shown on TV or streamed, such as the security check station, the mini stage for the red carpet emcee and the numerous media boxes located along the outer edge of the red carpet.

What TV and online viewers see is the last hour of the red carpet event. What fans most likely don't know is that attendees have been systematically flowing in for hours. The Dolby Theatre seats 3,400 people, and a majority of invitees enter via red carpet, but clearly it would be problematic to shuffle thousands of people within an hour of red carpet TV programming. The guests' appearances are scheduled according to nomination rank, meaning the nominees for best actor and actress (lead and supporting) arrive last, and lesser-known nominees in categories like short film, arrive first. That means the popular celebrities are at the right place at the right time to be interviewed on live television versus being inside the theatre and already seated.

Many fans imagine the red carpet to be a one-way glamorous avenue that is a single thoroughfare where celebrities leisurely stroll past flashing cameras and inquisitive reporters; however, the reality is that there is a lot of stalling among multiply lanes of pedestrian traffic. The red carpet that leads up to the Dolby Theatre's grand staircase is very wide; it takes up several vehicular traffic lanes. Once Oscar invitees hit the main walkway, it's organized chaos. There are two main pedestrian paths on the red carpet that are distinctly different. A thin strip of the red carpet, closest to the fans in the bleachers, is roped off for corporate and community guests. For example, PwC is a corporate partner, and the company is given several seats for its staff and affiliates. Those PwC guests are ushered down this thin strip located on the outer edge of the red carpet.

The second area is intended for Oscar nominees, their entourage, presenters, AMPAS Board of Governors, studio executives, and executives from sponsoring companies. The width of this area is much wider, and the media are stationed alongside this area so nominees and other well-known celebrities can walk up for interviews. Usually ABC-TV journalists are located closest to the main entrance to talk with celebrities right before they walk in, and this is what you see on TV and online.

In this larger thoroughfare of the red carpet, attendees actually hang out, sometimes for hours. They typically don't walk straight through in a few minutes because they want to stay on the red carpet as long as possible. For example, some of the lesser-known nominees arrive much earlier than the A-listers because that's the way AMPAS scheduled them to arrive. These nominees have been known to hang out on the red carpet waiting to see or meet the big name stars. They stand in groups and circulate within the area repeatedly, slowly inching their way toward the main entrance, stretching out their red carpet experience as long as possible.

Sometimes VIPs on the larger thoroughfare walk back and forth on the red carpet, too. They'll walk the path nearly to the end, then they'll walk back to the halfway point. They may stop to chat with media and other attendees, or they may circulate among the groups of people hanging out. It's like a networking event without food or drinks.

In years past, fans in bleacher seats located along the red carpet have the best view because they can see who's coming. Since the seats are on risers, fans have more of an ariel view than reporters on the ground and can see who is about to make an entrance. The bigger the celebrity, the louder the cheering. For many years, up to 700 fans were in the bleacher section, now there are approximately 100 individuals along the red carpet. The stars wave to fans and sometimes stop to take pictures with fans. There is also a red carpet emcee located directly across from the fan area who interviews celebrities, nominees, and presenters as they approach. A microphone and speakers are set up so that fans can hear the on-the-spot interviews. Fans can see other interviews on the red carpet taking place, they just can't hear what is being said.

Scheduling the Date

There have been a couple of times when the show couldn't go on and the ceremony was rescheduled. Three major national incidents occurred causing AMPAS to reschedule the date of the Oscars. The first ceremony to be rescheduled was the 41st Academy Awards in 1968 when Dr. Martin Luther King Jr. was killed. The Oscars were originally scheduled to take place on April 8, and Dr. King's funeral was April 9. AMPAS moved the Oscars to April 10. The other situation was in 1981 when President Ronald Reagan was shot and wounded. All major television networks were focused on that story, and AMPAS recognized that news coverage took precedence, so the show was rescheduled. The third was in 2021, when COVID-19 was considered a health risk to large crowds of people.

Currently, ABC-TV broadcasts the Oscars, so AMPAS works with them on scheduling a date for the Academy Awards. Typically, the event occurs the last Sunday of February or the first

Sunday of March. Depending upon what programs ABC already has lined up, like football games, the date can waver. If the Academy Awards don't take their usual Sunday spot, there are ripple effects. Date changes affect campaigning efforts for the filmmakers. A shift from the traditional date also affects film festivals and other awards programs, which have to be cognizant not to plan their events on the same weekend.

BEHIND THE SCENES

It takes hundreds of people working the Academy Awards to make the event flow smoothly. Not all the hired help are AMPAS staff members. A majority of people have been hired just for the event, which entails a lot of hustle before, during, and after. Here are some of the major roles that are performed on the big day. These are not the exact job titles, but something close.

Fan Seat Manager

There can't be a red carpet without a crowd of fans, so people who have been selected in a random drawing for AMPAS's fan seats fill the area alongside the red carpet to cheer on celebrities. The manager responsible for creating the fan crowd coordinates a security check for individuals months in advance. Then, when they all show up at 8 a.m. on Oscar Sunday, the manager and his or her team keeps them entertained throughout the day and provides meals until the red carpet fanfare starts. After all the nominees have made their way into the Dolby Theatre, the manager has the fans escorted to a nearby theatre to watch the Oscar telecast, where dinner and dessert are served.

Valet Manager

Coordinating drop-offs at the Oscars is a major production. The arrival times for approximately 700 vehicles are scheduled by a valet manager to ensure an orderly flow of vehicular and pedestrian traffic. There is a designated drop-off spot, where the red carpet begins, where limo drivers stop to let attendees out. There is a team of people who run over to the arriving limos to open the doors and let guests get out. Thereafter, the limo drivers head to a specific parking area nearby where they wait all night until guests are ready to leave.

Security Chief

Weeks before the event, security details begin when plans are made to close adjacent roads to the venue. On the day of the event, the head of security has already arranged for concrete roadblocks and the disbursement of Los Angeles Police officers. FBI and Department of Homeland Security personnel lock down the area to assist sniper officers on building rooftops and bomb-sniffing dogs. Some of the ushers on the red carpet and some patrons in the fan area along the red carpet are undercover officers.

Announcer's Voice

Inside the venue, there is a person who relays information overhead to inform attendees about commercial breaks and anecdotal information about winners. The person who plays the role of the "Voice of God" is not seated inside the Dolby; he or she is located in a trailer outside.

Wardrobe Repairers

There is a team of people carrying around small sewing kits to assist presenters and nominees in the case of a wardrobe or jewelry emergency. There is always one wardrobe mistress located behind the stage ready to do whatever is necessary to clean a stain, repair a necklace or fix a high-heeled shoe. Since the venue is so large, there are approximately seven wardrobe stations located throughout the Dolby Theatre.

Seat Fillers

With numerous cameras inside the Dolby Theatre aimed at

nominees sitting in the orchestra section, it's important that it always looks like a full house. Seat fillers are people dressed in formal attire who sit in empty seats when nominees get up and leave the area. This job was brought to light when Neil Patrick Harris was host in 2015 and walked around the first few rows looking for seat fillers.

Accountants

The spotlight was on these roles in 2017 when a PwC accountant gave the presenters the wrong envelope to announce the best picture winner. At the event, accountants from PwC transport the winning envelopes in a briefcase, and they're responsible for distributing the envelopes to the presenters backstage before the presenters go onstage. Their new protocol includes:

- Stage managers and presenters are to confirm they have been given the correct envelope by the PwC employee, before the presenters go onstage.
- A PwC employee has memorized the all the winners and has a complete set of winning envelopes. This person is in the control room with show's producers during the Oscars ceremony.
- All PwC employees performing these tasks rehearse potential mishaps.
- No PwC employees may use their mobile phone or social media during the show.

AWARD RECIPIENTS

When studios submit their films for consideration, key personnel are identified for every category, which is backed by the movie's credits. The Academy's rules state how many people can receive an Oscar statuette, and that figure differs by category. For categories where only one person is an eligible nominee, like best leading actress, the number of award recipients is obvious. When a winner is announced and a small group of people appear on stage, things are not so obvious. The information below describes who gets the award, according to AMPAS's 2023 rules and eligibility guidelines, for categories that don't naturally imply who is taking home an Oscar statuette.

Best Picture Award

The producer, not the director, is the person who brings all the elements of a movie together. It's a difficult job, and typically there are numerous producers who work on a film. But an Oscar statuette isn't given to everyone with the word "producer" in their job title. When a movie wins best picture, the individuals identified with "producer" or "produced by" in a film's credits will receive an Oscar. People who are credited as executive producer, co-producer, associate producer, line producer, or any other job that includes "producer" in its title will not get a statuette.

No more than three producers can be identified for this category. AMPAS does consider a team of two individuals as a single producer only when the Producers Guild of America's Producing Partnership Panel has validated the bona fide producing partnership. In addition, the PGA must have determined the producer eligible for a PGA Award for the movie. If not, then the producers must have appealed to the PGA for refusal of eligibility.

Animated Feature Film Award

The award recipients are a combination of directors and producers. There must be at least one director and one person credited in a producer's role. There can be up to four individuals named; however, they must be the people who are most responsible for the creative portion and overall achievement of the film. The director credit must be director, not co-director. The individuals identified as producer must have been credited in the film as "producer" or "produced by" in order to receive an Oscar, not as executive producers, co-producers, associate producers, line producers, and so on. The same PGA qualifications apply here.

International Feature Film Award

Unfortunately, the producers don't get an Oscar for this category as they do in the best picture category; the director does. Basically, the director may accept the award on behalf of the creative team, and the actual inscription on the statuette will have the originating country, the film's title, and the director's name.

Documentary Feature Film Award

This is another category that awards directors and producers with an Oscar statuette. Up to three people can be named, and they must have been equally responsible for key creative aspects. One individual must be a credited director and another individual as a credited director or producer. The producer has to meet AMPAS's criteria for that role, and the same guidelines apply as stated in other categories.

Documentary Short Film Award

This category can distribute up to two Oscars and are given to the one or two individuals who were most involved in the creative process of making the movie. One person must be the credited director, and the second individual, if applicable, can be a director or producer. If a producer is named, that person is vetted by AMPAS.

Animated and Live Action Short Film Awards

AMPAS appears to be a little more flexible in this category, as a maximum of two awards can be given to the people who are the most responsible for the concept and the creative execution of the film. One must be an accredited director and the other must be a person is a key creative role. It is up to the filmmakers to decide in advance who will go on stage to accept the statuettes.

Live Action Short Film Awards

Slightly different guidelines apply to these award winners. A maximum of two awards can be given, and the requirement is for one credited director and the other award can be given to a credited writer, producer or another director. If a producer is named, then he/she role must align with AMPAS producers criteria.

Original Score Award

This is for the person who creates entirely new music for the whole movie. It's an enormous task and up to two Oscar statuettes can be awarded. AMPAS expects one person to take credit for the film's music; however, if two composers contributed equally, then each person receives an Oscar for the winning film. If there are three or more collaborators, then a single Oscar will be awarded to the group.

Original Song Award

This award is for the song writers, and the status quo is two statuettes; however, up to four can be awarded under extraordinary circumstances. If there are three individuals who contributed equally, then three Oscars are awarded. It's rare that four statuettes are given; however, there can be extenuating circumstances and the Music Branch Executive Committee has the authority to grant an exception to the norm. If the writers are an actual musical group, then only one award is given.

Makeup and Hairstyling Award

It typically takes a team of makeup artists and hairstyling artists to achieve a character's look, so there can be up to three statuettes given for this category. There is usually a lead member for each team, hence the Oscar goes to the three individuals who are primarily responsible for this craft.

VIEWERSHIP

There has been a decades-long opinion that if popular films were nominated, then more people would watch the Academy Awards. Well, that time finally came and the results were unremarkable.

The theory that Oscar viewership will naturally increase if popular films are nominated was finally put to the test in 2019. Marvel's film, *Black Panther,* was nominated for best picture, along with blockbusters *A Star is Born* and *Bohemian Rhapsody,* and Academy Award viewership increased by 12 percent. In 2019, there were 29.6 million viewers, and in 2018, 26.5 million people watched the awards ceremony.

The host is partially responsible for attracting viewers, so its interesting there was an increase in 2019 with a hostless show. Do you know which host had the highest-ranking Academy Awards telecast? That claim to fame belongs to Billy Crystal. In 1998, he hosted when *Titanic* won best picture, and 57.25 million viewers saw the telecast on ABC-TV. Maybe the draw that year was Leonardo DiCaprio or Kate Winslet. Whatever it was, it worked, because viewership has fluctuated thereafter. The ceremony in 2018 was the lowest-rated Oscars ceremony, garnering only 26.5 million viewers. The very first telecast in 1953 reached 40 million viewers, and back then, only three major networks existed.

AMPAS and ABC-TV have agreed to partner on Academy Awards telecasts until 2028. The nonprofit gets a large percentage of the estimated $162 million in annual revenue. The television outlet may offer bonuses for benchmark viewership numbers, and the two entities are continually coming up with ideas on how to increase the number of people who watch, particularly ages 18–49. The challenge is coming up with ways to engage people with the live event when they have numerous other viewing choices that don't involve commercials. Another hurdle is the length of the ceremony, which ranges from two-to-three hours. Tactics to shorten the ceremony failed to boost viewership, and the cuts angered industry professionals when a few categories were omitted from the televised portion of the show.

The Corona Virus pandemic had some effect on viewership, lowering it to 9.85 million in 2021 and 15.6 million in 2022, Although the pandemic hit in 2020, the Oscars ceremony had already taken place February 9, 2020, with 23.6 million viewers, it was just before the pandemic caused a total shutdown in the U.S. on March 15, 2020. Although viewership increased to 18.76 million in 2023, drawing audiences to the show is a constant challenge, especially when viewers have an overwhelming number of other media to watch.

GOVERNORS BALL

When the Academy Awards conclude, the winners, nominees, presenters, and a select group of approximately 1,500 people are invited to the AMPAS Governors Ball, the official Oscars after party. The event takes place at the Dolby Theatre in an adjacent ballroom, and it's where winners have their Oscar statuettes plated with an inscription of their accomplishment.

AMPAS has been hosting this event since 1958, and it's usually the first post-party station for nominees and their guests, VIPs, sponsors and AMPAS members that night. Every year, there is a designated theme, and professional party planners work with AMPAS members to carry it out through elegant decor, live music, and imaginative gourmet food and beverages. The party venue is transformed into a wonderland where guests browse different stations located throughout the room to experience all that is being offered.

Legendary chef Wolfgang Puck has been the culinary mastermind for the Governors Ball for more than two decades. His team of 900 is responsible for developing one-of-a-kind dishes and incorporating the party's theme into the menu. In 2023, some delicacies included beet Napoleon salad, crispy Moroccan lamb cigar, and confit golden beet with cashew crème and gastrique mint. Desserts included raspberry and lemon sable breton tart, hazelnut and salted caramel praline Paris brest, and ube and calamansi entremet cake In 2019, some of the delicacies were Nashville-style hot fried quail on a red velvet waffle; vegan torchio pasta with arugula, tomato, and caper berries; and heirloom carrot "tartare." Desserts included matcha cherry macarons, square pillow cake with coconut mango and passion fruit, and a black forest "cherry" small plate. The annual favorites are smoked salmon in the shape of an Oscar statuette and 24K gold dusted chocolate Oscars. The favorite dishes for returning guests are the chicken pot pie and the brick oven pizzas. All is served with the official champagne of the Academy Awards, Golden Piper Heidsieck.

AMPAS shares its party plans with the media by releasing fun facts about the Governors Ball Some of the interesting details revealed in the preview are the event menu, illustrated renderings and pictures of the decor, plans for the floral design, and plans for incorporating locally sourced organic foods. There are also interesting fun facts, like having a 2,600-pound sculpted ice bar, making 6,500 wood-fired Oscar-shaped flat breads, and placing 600 candles in gold and sparkling crystal containers. No doubt, this soiree is opulent.

The plaquing of the Oscar statuettes with winners' names is the most important activity that occurs at the Governors Ball. Basically, the Oscars are given to the winners without a label, and when winners arrive at the ball, they head over to where the engravers are located. Winners hand over their statuettes so an engraver can attach a plaque identifying the award they just won. First, the engraver has the statuette's serial number documented. Then the engraver inscribes the winner's name on the plaque which already has the award category on it. Before the plaque is mounted onto the Oscar, the winner sees the inscriptions to confirm the information is correct. Then the engraver screws the plaque onto the statuette, gives it a quick polish, then gently gives it back to the new Academy Award recipient.

OSCAR PARTIES

There are special events that occur days before the Academy Awards, and of course, there are after parties. Admission to most is by invitation only, and those that make tickets available to the public charge a mint. Usually, the studios and film-related organizations host honoree-type events the week before the Oscars, and celebrities host ultra-private after parties where no cameras are allowed.

Studios whose films have been nominated, such as Netflix and Warner Brothers, host a pre-Oscar party to celebrate an anticipated win. By this time, all the votes have been submitted, so studio groups sit back, relax and celebrate their achievements. There are also numerous organizations that host events to honor a specific demographic working in film. These are some of the annual independent events that happen the week of the Academy Awards in Los Angeles.

Global Green's Annual Pre-Oscar Party

Global Green USA hosts a gala to raise funds and awareness for their programs. It's the only gala with a green carpet, and it's attended by eco-minded celebrities who support sustainability strategies, environmental policy, affordable housing, and correcting climate change.

Annual Oscar Wilde Awards

The U.S. Ireland-Alliance honors entertainment industry professionals at its annual event. The organization is a nonprofit dedicated to solidifying existing relationships between the United States and Ireland. Some of its honorees include Glenn Close, Melissa McCarthy, Martin Short, and Mark Hamill. For the past several years, J.J. Abrams has served as emcee.

Cadillac Oscar Party

As the official Academy Awards sponsor who transports nominees and VIPs to the Oscars, Cadillac hosts a pre-awards event. Numerous A-listers and nominees have attended, such as Zoe Saldana, Naomi Watts, Christoph Waltz, and Barry Jenkins.

Annual Women in Film Pre-Oscar Cocktail Party

This event is typically hosted by a female A-lister, and the women who have been nominated for an Academy Award are honored and recognized. Generous sponsors include Max Mara and Lancôme.

Talent Agency Parties

Agencies like Creative Artist Agency (CAA) and United Talent Agency (UTA) host parties for their clients who have been nominated for an Academy Award. Most parties take place at a private location.

On Oscar Night, there are numerous private events in Los Angeles that are mainly to view the Academy Awards. Some organizers use the occasion as an invitation-only fundraiser, while other viewing events are intended only for clients. Prominent viewing parties include:

- Mercedes Benz Oscars Viewing Party
- IMDb LIVE Viewing Party
- Byron Allen's Annual Entertainment Studios Oscar Gala

Regarding after parties, the one hosted by *Vanity Fair* is the most popular, and people bounce between that and other celebrity events. Elton John's AIDS Foundation event is just as well-known, and Jay-Z and Beyonce's Gold Party is gaining attention as a must-attend event. These events are known to have varying levels of access and VIP status. Attendees may be admitted through the door, but where they go from there may be limited if they don't have the right credentials.

CHAPTER 8 – DO OSCAR NIGHT RIGHT

It would be epic to attend the Academy Awards—wearing gorgeous formal attire, walking the red carpet, having your photograph taken looking like a million bucks. You might see Timothee Chalamet, Jennifer Lawrence, Michael B. Jordan, or spot Margot Robbie. But that's not going to happen. The Oscars are invitation only.

The Dolby Theatre has 3,400 seats. There are 10,000+ Academy members, so even if you are a member, chances are slim you'll score a ticket. But what if there were a way you could capture that magic? What if you could make this year's Oscars a standout for you? How could you step it up? Instead of being a mere Oscar viewer, you could operate like an Academy Awards insider.

There is more to the Academy Awards than walking the red carpet and attending fancy parties. This chapter will tell you how to do Oscar Night right. There are valuable resources that will excite, inspire, and engage you like never before. The information in this chapter will make this your best Oscar Season ever.

Reflect on the ceremony for a minute. It's usually three hours, meaning your Oscar fun only lasts for an evening. Maybe it spills into the next day, but generally speaking, the experience is short-lived. This chapter is going to change that. The Oscars are about movies, so we're stripping away all of the glitz and glamour (just for a moment), and getting right to the heart of the Academy Awards. We all love movies, and the films that have been nominated are being showcased as the crème de la crème of motion picture art. This chapter will help you explore this beautiful and compelling art form.

THREE-STEP PREP

This chapter isn't all about having an awesome Oscar party. It's about how to create an Academy Awards experience in your corner of the world. This book is like a GPS taking you on an Academy Awards adventure, and it'll reveal where to go and what to do, making this the best film journey you've ever been on. This is how you create a golden experience.

Step 1: Preparing for the Big Night
Step 2: Determining the Merit of Nominated Films
Step 3: Making Party Plans

For seasoned viewers, some of this information will seem fundamental. For new Oscar viewers, some of this information will be an overload. It's guaranteed that you will learn something new.

Step 1: Preparing for the Big Night

These activities are stepping stones on an Oscar journey you can do from home. Your excitement will definitely grow as the days leading up to the Academy Awards dwindle.

There are two types of go-to resources: internal resources and external resources.

Internal Resources

1. Official Websites

Check out these two different websites to get Academy Awards news and information direct from the source:

- www.oscars.org

  This website is populated by AMPAS and contains film resources, its awards database, and information about the nonprofit organization's history and awards programs.

- www.oscars.go.com

    This website is populated by ABC-TV and is focused on celebrity news, fashion, and red-carpet buzz.

2. Nominees List in a PDF

On the day the nominees are announced, AMPAS releases a beautifully formatted PDF containing the complete list of the nominees that can be downloaded from www.oscars.go.com.

This list has the nominees for all 23 categories. All the categories have five nominees, except best picture. There are 10 nominees for best picture. At the actual event, the awards are not given in the same order as they appear in the PDF.

3. Academy Conversations

The Academy has a YouTube channel with a playlist called Academy Conversations, and its a must-see for nominated films. When you learn the backstory about a film, you become part of a group of privileged individuals who know what went on behind the scenes to create the movie. At the Academy Conversations playlist, you'll find a panel of cast and crew members discussing their film's production.

Most of the videos on this playlist are films in the popular nomination categories, such as best picture, best director, best actor, and best actress. Your task is to see Academy Conversations for the nominated films you've seen.

External Resources

1. Subscribe to *The Hollywood Reporter*

Tap into the nomination buzz by subscribing to *The Hollywood Reporter* (THR), a weekly industry magazine. Read the articles online for free or follow them on social media. You can also pay $100 to get an annual hardcopy subscription. The publication has articles from top-notch award analysts and film critics. Expect to see articles like "Who Will Win vs. Who Should Win" and "My Brutally Honest Oscar Ballot." There's even an Oscar edition, which is a great keepsake.

2. Follow Movie Award Pundits

In addition to following The Academy on social media, there are others pushing out content consistently during Oscar season. In no particular order, check out these outlets on social platforms: The Hollywood Reporter's @AwardsChatter, The LA Times' "The Envelope," The New York Times' "The Projectionist," People magazine, Entertainment Weekly magazine, and Sasha Stone @AwardsDaily,

Follow me on Facebook @CRLesterAuthor and X (formerlyTwitter) @CLesterPR to get all the latest on creating an exceptional fan experience. I relay information about contests for fans, fun activities to do at your viewing party, pro tips and the secrets about the Oscars that are surprising and beneficial movie fans, film scholars and independent filmmakers.

3.. Watch the Oscar Documentary

See *And the Oscar Goes To* (2014) documentary. It's very entertaining and highly educational, so make it a permanent part of your annual prep work. The history lesson relayed in the film gives viewers the inside scoop about the Academy Awards' early beginnings, a peek at some of the turbulent times, the backstory from former hosts, and commentary from individuals who won.

Step 2: Determining a Film's Merit

Members of AMPAS have the privilege of nominating films they believe demonstrate excellence in motion picture art and science. After the nominations have been made, their job is to see all the movies in approximately three to four weeks so that they can vote accordingly. Now, it's time for you to be in the judge's seat. This Oscar Season, select one category from the list of 23 and see all the films for that category to determine a winner.

I. Select a Category

Your mission, if you choose to accept it, is to select one category from the list of 23, then see all the films nominated for that category. There is a high level of integrity and authenticity to this challenge. You've got to put aside your prejudices against the kinds of movies you don't like.

Artistically and culturally, it's more difficult than you might think because you're stepping outside your comfort zone. But that's what makes for an enriching Academy Awards experience.

There are three requirements for this mission:

a. You must see all the films in that category, even if they're a genre you typically don't like.

b. You must watch the entire movie, no matter what.

c. You must see them all before Oscar Night. Whether a movie is about an astronaut going to the moon or catfighting British royals from the 1700s, you've got to watch it. Select a category now.

II. Determining a film's merit

It would be cumbersome to analyze every film's elements (up to 23 components), so make it easy on yourself by critiquing a few key factors. Use these simple qualifiers to help develop a broader perspective and an informed opinion about the movies up for an Oscar.

- *Acting*: Movies have prominent and interesting characters with definite motives. Your job is to determine if the characters were believable as portrayed by the actors and actresses.
- *Story*: Whether the film is animated or live action, your job is to determine if the story is clear and cohesive. Did the action sequence make sense, or were there holes in the storyline?
- *Production*: Consider all the components that went into the film (e.g., the level of complexity to shoot footage on a mountaintop, the number of extras in a scene, the costumes, camera angles, the time period of the story, and so on).
- *Impact*: Was it thought-provoking? Was there something about the film that compelled you to think about it after you saw it? Did something stick with you hours or

days later? Did it get your mind going?

- *Emotion*: Was there an emotional touch? If you laughed hysterically or cried like a baby, or if you had any other strong reaction to a film, you were emotionally touched.
- *Worthiness*: Will You See It Again? The mark of a great movie is one you are willing to pay to see again. Connecting with films on a personal level is possible, and those that resonate with you are the ones you can see repeatedly.

Viewing Protocol

Before you go out to go see movies, these are the expectations as you judge Academy Award nominees. Think of these as the rules of engagement.

Give your best when watching films.
Watch films at a time of day when you're alert and have energy. Don't sabotage your efforts by seeing movies when you're fatigued or sleepy. It's preferred that you see movies at the theater so you can have a holistic experience but, whether you're in a theater or on your sofa streaming a flick, really be present to appreciate what the film has to offer. Eliminate distractions. Don't multitask.

Try not to go in with preconceived notions. Dismiss the opinions of others who have seen films you haven't. You want your viewing experience to be untainted and untarnished, so don't let the opinions of others ruin it for you.

Stay for the credits.
One of the most important parts of a movie is recognizing the people who worked on the film. Invest a few more minutes in the movie by staying for the credits. It's interesting to see the number of individuals, sometimes in the hundreds, who worked on it. By seeing the credits, you'll learn where it was filmed, what musical artists were involved, and other interesting things you hadn't considered as movie elements. Did you know the caterer that provides the cast and crew meals is included in the credits?

Space out viewings.

This is not the time to binge watch. Definitely do not watch several films in a day. Watch one or two, maybe three movies max, within a week, a couple of days apart. Like fine wine poured from a newly opened bottle, wait a bit before you consume. Sometimes a great film will stick with you for hours, even days after you've seen it. Movies trigger our emotions, so don't overload yourself by viewing several films in one day. Binge watching is not recommended.

Step 3: Making Party Plans

You already know the date and the basic agenda: the red carpet arrivals happen first, then the ceremony commences thereafter. First, determine the type of party you want to host. Whether it is a private party for two or a gathering for a gregarious group, plan to celebrate Hollywood's biggest night with others. The ceremony is more fun with like-minded individuals, so reach out to your movie mates and make a go of it.

Next, determine the style of party. Make it as informal or formal as you want because the most important thing here is to have fun celebrating movies. The menu can be whatever you want: pot luck, pizza, or recipes by renowned Oscars caterer Wolfgang Puck.

I. Have Fun Keeping Track

The agenda for the big night is typically the same every year. Typically, the actress in a supporting role is the first category winner to be announced, and the best picture is the last. Have fun with all the action that happens in between. For example, rate acceptance speeches with a thumb's up or down, tally how many winners say, "It's a dream come true," or make note of a common political or social justice message.

After you've made your predictions, there are two ways you can keep track of the winners that will keep your excitement on high: by film and by category. Using a nominee list as your guide, make a list of the films with the most nominations, and keep track of how many awards those films garner. Create a scoreboard and display it for all to see how the numbers add up for the heavily weighted films.

Next, use your nomination guide that has your choices, and note the winners as they are announced for each category. During the commercial breaks, tally both lists to see how things are progressing.

II. Generate Good Vibes

One of the best parts of the ceremony is seeing your favorite famous peeps present or perform at the event. It's like seeing dear friends whom you love and adore, so feel free to cheer for them. Throw confetti, blow a horn, tap a soundbite on your phone, or post hearts on social media when your loved ones appear on the screen. The same applies when your nominee-of-choice wins.

There is a solemn time in the ceremony when "In Memoriam" appears. Photographs of notable industry professionals who have died within the past year are displayed to honor their contributions to filmmaking. Light a candle and take this time to remember them and any of your favorite celebrities and filmmakers who have passed. Feel free to raise a glass and toast in their honor.

Lastly, keep that good energy flowing until the very end! Why is that important? Something could go terribly wrong, and you don't want to miss out on all of the drama.

SWAG

The best accessories for an Academy Awards party, formal or not, are gifts. Oscars ceremony guests get swag bags, and your guests should, too! Create your own swag to give attendees at your viewing event. Mention the goodies during your party, but wait until the ceremony is over to pass them out. Here are some gift suggestions, so be sure to prepare in advance.

Exclusive Fan Guides

Cinephiles love the inside scoop, so gift them with my series of books for Oscar fans. They'll learn and love all four fan guides. A complete list is on the last page. (Amazon.com for the book series)

Oscar Cookies

Make sugar cookies using a mummy cookie cutter, and dust with gold sprinkles. Put each one in a clear bag and tie with a gold ribbon (Amazon.com for cookie cutter).

Oscar Coffee Mug

Give your guests a branded coffee mug filled with fancy candy or gourmet coffee packets. Friends will remember the event with every sip (academymuseum.org).

Movie Note Pack

Everyone is a film critic, and gifting a branded AMPAS pocket film notes journal and branded Oscars pen helps film fans keep their thoughts on paper (academymuseum.org).

Awards Program

This is a unique giveaway and keepsake because it's the official event program that is given to Academy Awards attendees (academymuseum.org).

PLAN FOR NEXT YEAR

The Oscars are an annual event, and AMPAS announces its ceremony dates on its website years in advance. Now that you know when Oscar Season starts and the sequence of events, it's easy to plan ahead.

The Academy posts very little information about Oscar Season. Although the organization has a fiscal year, they don't publicly acknowledge the start and end date of Oscar Season like the entertainment industry does; its occurrence is unofficial yet broadly accepted by professionals in the film industry. To help you prepare for the next season, put these tasks on your calendar.

September

Oscar Season launches on Labor Day weekend. Research Telluride Film Festival, Venice Film Festival, Toronto International Film Festival and the other festivals mentioned in Chapter 1.

November

Movie awards begin in mid-fall. Be on the lookout for the Gotham Awards, Screen Actors Guild (SAG) Award, the Governors Awards, Golden Globe and ceremony dates for the other awards programs mentioned in Chapter 2.

December

Academy Award announces short lists for select categories. Out of hundreds of eligible films, AMPAS reveals a short list of films now under serious consideration for an Oscar.

January

One of the most important dates of Oscar Season—after months of speculation, the nominees are finally revealed.

February or March

Oscar ceremony occurs in late winter. This date is also announced months in advance in AMPAS's "key dates" press release and is included in other related press releases.

When it comes to the Academy Awards, Oscar Season is just the tip of the iceberg. There is so much information available to the public that most fans don't know exists. Be sure to read this guide's companion books outlined on the next page.

ABOUT THE AUTHOR

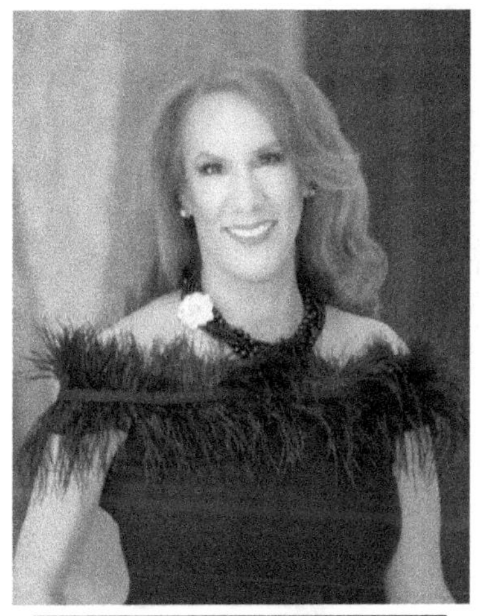

Photo by Tammy Lechner

Catherine R. Lester is a diehard Oscar fan devoted to guiding others through an enriching Academy Awards experience. She's discovered the inside scoop about golden opportunities that most fans don't know exist. Having researched, studied, and validated riveting resources, most of which are public offerings from the Academy of Motion Picture Arts and Sciences, Catherine has created this step-by-step guide that takes readers through Oscar Season.

Her goal for writing this book about Oscar Season is to inform film fans and independent filmmakers about the process Academy Award-hopefuls go through. Movie goers and movie makers will learn about the three major phases of Oscar Season, and will be well informed about Academy Award eligibility and guidelines. Readers will know how to catch the Oscar buzz well before Academy Award nominations are announced.

Catherine educates filmmakers and movie fans about the Academy Awards with the goal of getting them to the Oscars. Her four books are the only ones in existence that pave the way to the red carpet for everyday people. Having studied the Oscars for nearly three decades, she has in-depth knowledge that greatly benefits filmmakers and movie fans.

Her fan experience includes viewing every Academy Awards' best picture nominee since 1997 and attending the following Academy of Motion Picture Arts and Sciences public events: the grand opening of the Academy Museum of Motion Pictures, Oscar Night at the Museum, Oscar Red Carpet Fan Experience, Oscar Week, Oscar Concert, and Singin' in the Rain and Hollywood Costume in Los Angeles, and Oscar Roadtrip and Oscar Fan Experience in Texas. She is also a founding supporter of the Academy Museum of Motion Pictures and the author of three other guides for Oscar Fans:

Experience Oscar Week: Get in On Academy Awards Action

Academy Awards Excitement: How To Do Oscar Night Right

Inside the Academy Museum: Elevate Your Visitor Experience from Memorable to Transformational

She has a B.A. in Communications and is a member of Women In Film (WIF Los Angeles) and the American Film Institute (AFI).

Facebook: CRLesterAuthor
X: @CLesterPR
Website: www.crlesterauthor.com
Catherine Lester's YouTube channel. Fan Experience - Academy Awards playlist

---

Did you do Oscar Season using tips from this book? Post on social media and tag @CRLesterAuthor on Facebook or @CLesterPR on X.

RESOURCES

Academy of Motion Picture Arts and Sciences
www.oscars.org

ABC-TV's Oscars news and information
www.oscars.go.com

The Hollywood Reporter
www.thr.com

Billboard
www.billboard.com

www.ingramcontent.com/pod-product-compliance
Lightning Source LLC
LaVergne TN
LVHW020646100826
845148LV00012B/2350

* 9 7 8 0 5 7 8 6 2 4 5 2 5 *